The Other Side of Sorrow

The Other Side of Sorrow

*After the death of three-year-old Rachel,
God leads the grieving mother through guilt and anger
to healing and peace*

Sandy Derksen with Connie Nash

AUGSBURG Publishing House • Minneapolis

THE OTHER SIDE OF SORROW

Contents

Preface

Rachel Ann Derksen was born October 24, 1973, in Garkida, a village in Nigeria. She died at home in Fresno, California, on August 18, 1976. Five years have passed since that final earthly event for our young daughter. During that time, my husband, Wilf, and I have searched to find healing for our wounds.

That healing has come, but our grieving has been a process, a process that is different for each person. For myself I discovered that a certain amount of determination to face the loss and a willingness to go through the sorrow was necessary for me to find healing.

There will be other deaths, other sorrows for us; we all face them at some time in our lives. Children are not always ours to hold for long. Relationships grow and change. Jobs, places, treasures of many kinds are not guaranteed forever.

I do not welcome loss, yet I have learned not to run from it. Wilf and I have learned that healing awaits our decision to level with ourselves, with God, and with others.

Perhaps some aspect of this book will relate to your story, and we will meet on that common ground. My hope is that you who read this book will find healing for a wound still open, not by justifying the event that caused it, nor by ignoring the painful feelings that surround it, but by walking through that sorrow, with eyes open, to the other side. For us it became a path to joy.

I would like to thank Charlyn Bridges for her help in organizing this book; my husband, Wilf, for his many hours of sharing and encouragement; and the many family members and friends who prayed for us in our time of sorrow and who prayed for us during the writing of this book. A special thanks to Connie Nash for her ability to help me express this story in writing. Besides being close as a sister, she has become my dearest friend.

1

Rachel

Wilf was seeing patients at the medical center when the alert sounded on his portable pager. "Dr. Derksen," the operator sounded alarmed, "I'm holding an urgent call for you from your neighbor Susie. Please hurry!" Wilf reached for a nearby phone thinking, as if to reassure himself, *Sandy and neighbors have called before in panic for things that were quite easy to handle.*

Susie's voice was hurried and urgent but under control. "Wilf, Rachel fell into our swimming pool and we need you immediately!"

"I'll be right there!" Wilf answered and slammed the receiver down. He stood motionless for a few seconds, hoping Susie's urgency was undue alarm. "John," he turned to another physician, "an emergency has happened at my home. I need to leave now."

The hospital was less than a mile from home, and Wilf had walked to work that day. He debated for a moment whether to borrow someone's car or run home. By then he was beginning to sense that something desperate had happened. He charged down the hospital stairs and sprinted into the street. He was about halfway home when his pager sounded again. "Dr. Derksen, the ambulance is bringing your daughter. Please come back to the hospital."

By this time Wilf was numb with panic. Realizing something terrible had happened to Rachel, he turned around and headed toward the hospital. He entered the emergency room with hot sweat rolling off his flushed and drawn face. He grabbed the nearest nurse. "Get the big room ready! We have a drowning coming in for resuscitation! It's my daughter!" He was still breathing heavily.

An emergency room doctor calmly took hold of Wilf's arm. "We're all ready. We know it's your daughter, Wilf. The operator called us. Everything is waiting."

Wilf was relieved to know that the hospital staff was prepared, but anxiety whitened his face. He walked to the exit, looking nervously down the street for signs of the ambulance. "What's taking them so long?" he asked frantically. "I should have kept running home!"

———◆———

I relived that day a thousand times. The morning had been ordinary enough. . . .

"Let's get up, everybody!" The delicious, groggy silence was shattered, as usual, by our authoritative three-year-old daughter. Bleary-eyed, I smiled at Rachel, our firstborn, whose straight blonde hair and big blue eyes were dancing.

"Where's Daddy?"

I listened; the rest of the house was quiet. "He must have left for work already. Want to come snuggle?"

She climbed in with me and ruffled my hair. I played with her round tummy. We teased and hugged. I was grateful that one-year-old Phillip was still sleeping. There is a certain joy in one child at a time.

Finally I persuaded myself to get out of bed and was just confronting an awesome pile of laundry when the front doorbell rang. "I'll get it, Mommy!" Rachel had learned to turn the large antique doorknob. She loved to be grown-up.

Five-year-old Kimberly from next door rushed in. "Rachel, my daddy just finished the pool! Can you come play in it with me?"

Large-eyed, my daughter listened to her best friend. Then they both looked at me hopefully.

"Not now; I'll go with you later, Rachel."

"It's just a little pool," Kimberly pleaded.

"Please, Mommy?" There was that characteristic perplexed line in Rachel's brow, just like her father's.

"Later today, Rachel."

Kimberly left with reluctant acceptance.

While Phillip played intently with his blocks and Rachel sat on the drainboard "helping" me dry dishes, I thought of various activities to fill the summer and match my children's limitless energy.

Summertime was visiting the San Joaquin Valley, and I was glad for the timeliness of the sunken wading pool. Two days earlier the children and I had watched its construction in progress. Kimberly's father, Jim, set bricks around the pool area to give it a nice, aesthetic border. As I had watched him work carefully, I anticipated the laughter and fun that would soon fill their backyard.

A washload later, Kimberly was back again to see if Rachel could play at her house. When I agreed, Rachel energetically skipped out the front door. A half hour had passed when Rachel returned and dashed upstairs to her room. She quickly came down again, carrying a large white purse. "What's in your purse?" I asked.

"Toys. I want Kimberly to see," Rachel replied, prancing out the door. I followed her.

Susie, Kimberly's pretty mother, a petite young woman with long dark hair, was watering her front lawn. "Hi, Rachel!" she said. "You must have great plans with your big white bag!" Rachel nodded, eyes big with imagination.

Susie looked up and saw me. I waved from the front porch, then returned inside to attend to the laundry. I was glad to have someone like Susie with whom to share child care. I appreciated her perceptive, thoughtful way with Phillip, Rachel, and her own two girls. We would sometimes sit together in one of our adjoining backyards and watch the children play. It was good to be in the company of another adult. A close relationship was beginning to develop between us.

I put sleepy Phillip in his bed for a nap and cleared the toys spread across the family room, but I could not shake a deep fatigue. Wilf and I had planned to celebrate our wedding anniversary that night. I loved going out and had looked forward to this rare evening alone together, but I was exhausted. I dialed the pediatric clinic at the medical center where Wilf was finishing his residency. "I just don't feel like going out tonight," I told him. "Would you mind waiting a few days?" He sounded disappointed but admitted that he was tired as well and agreed to wait.

Trying to feel better, I washed my hair. As I was drying it, the doorbell rang. It was Kimberly again.

"Where's Rachel?"

"Over at your house."

"No, she isn't."

"But haven't you just been playing with her?"

"No, I've been at Tiffany's."

"She must be playing with your little sister at your house."

"No! I just looked!"

I was sure she had not looked enough. But just to satisfy a bit of doubt as to where Rachel might be, I decided that the two of us should look together. We visited the nearby play spots first. While in our backyard, I glanced over the fence into Kimberly's yard. No one was there. I was sure that my daughter was in Kimberly's house, probably playing with Jodi. "Why don't you see if she's in your house now," I advised Kimberly, "and tell me when you find her."

I went back inside my house. While upstairs, I was suddenly filled with fear. I ran down the stairs toward our front door. Then I heard Susie scream. I knew Rachel had been found—in the pool.

As I neared the pool, I was horrified to see Rachel, purplish-blue, lying limp at its side. Her wet orange shorts and white T-shirt were clinging to her. I bent down and immediately cleared her airway, then began mouth-to-mouth resuscitation. *She's going to be all right,* I kept telling myself, but I could not find a heartbeat. *I need help!*

"Susie, call Wilf!" Panic ran through me. "Get an ambulance!"

Ron Adams, a neighbor, was suddenly there, feeling for Rachel's heartbeat. As he knelt beside me and pushed on her chest, I continued breathing puffs of air into her mouth. Frantically I asked, "Ron, is there a heartbeat?"

He shook his head.

"It's too late! Maybe we should quit!"

"No, Sandy, keep trying. Her color is better."

A panorama of memories flooded my mind and senses. I remembered, as a nurse, resuscitating a newborn baby. I recalled Rachel fainting after one of her breath-holding spells. *Just keep at it,* I told myself. *She'll come through this time too.*

It seemed an eternity before the paramedics came. Finally we sped into the hospital emergency entrance. Wilf was stunned when he saw Rachel. He practically tore her out of the medic's arms. I saw terror in his face. A nurse screamed at him, "Keep pushing on her chest! I'll breathe for her. Easy, let's take her in carefully."

I felt helpless just watching, but there was nothing now that I could do. Wilf's pale, shocked face began to fill with

14

determination. I knew his medical training was winning over panic. I breathed more easily as I followed them into the emergency room.

Wilf and another doctor directed the rescuscitation. A tube was placed in Rachel's windpipe and an intravenous line was inserted into her arm. Lifesaving drugs were administered through the vein, and oxygen was pumped into her lungs. Wilf's hands were steady now as he worked over her still, bluish body.

"Her pupils are fixed and dilated," a nurse stated.

"How long was she under—does anyone know?" the other doctor asked.

"About 10 minutes," I guessed and burst into tears. "Oh, I don't know!"

Someone touched me gently.

"Another half vial of bicarb, please!" Wilf was strangely calm as he continued pushing on Rachel's chest.

I knew I had to leave and stumbled through my tears onto a cushioned chair just outside the emergency room. "God, don't let her die!" I sobbed quietly.

Wilf finally pushed open the emergency room door. I stood up and reached for him, my eyes stinging with fear. We held each other tightly and were silent. Neither of us could find words. Finally he whispered, "How long? How long was she under?"

"I don't know!" I answered with frustration. "Wilf, how is she?"

"Well, her heart is beating now and she's breathing with the help of the respirator."

"Is she going to live?"

"I—I—we don't know," Wilf answered. Then his voice lost its calm in his tears. I knew he was struggling to comfort me and to understand, but he was Rachel's father. I squeezed his arms and turned to see Susie and Jim walking into the waiting room. There was no color in Susie's face, and her lovely eyes were large and staring with horror.

"Sandy, she's dead! She's dead! How can you forgive me!" She sobbed uncontrollably.

"No, she's not dead. Rachel's going to live, Susie." I hugged her. Wilf embraced us both. Then he spoke gently but firmly. "I want both of you to go home now. Come back in an hour. She will be in the intensive care unit by that time." He took a deep breath. "It's going to be a long wait."

2

Hope

About seven-thirty that evening, Wilf's brother, Lloyd, sister, Beverly, and parents arrived at the hospital. Together we went into the intensive care unit (ICU). Rachel's chest moved up and down as a mechanical respirator breathed for her. She was comatose and made no spontaneous movements. Her eyes were closed.

Wilf was controlled as he tried to explain her condition. "We are not sure how much injury her brain has suffered from lack of oxygen while she lay in the pool. If she wakes up in the next 24 to 48 hours, we can be quite confident that she will be OK." His family members were all silent and stunned as they listened.

"She will be supported with the respirator and intravenous fluids," he added. "Everything possible is being done. In the meantime we just have to wait and pray that God will bring her through this."

We were quiet. There was nothing more to say. Memories of a recent family get-together focused in my mind. Members of Wilf's family had gathered for a weekend of fun at his parents' home. One evening we heartily consumed a picnic of homemade sausage and rolls. We laughed and swapped stories and argued over politics, interrupting each other frequently—a typical Derksen tradition. Later, Mom Derksen summed up our thoughts in her strong, quiet way: "God has certainly blessed our family. . . ."

As I looked at Rachel, now motionless under the hospital apparatus, those words hung in my mind without joy. Searching the sober faces around our usually exuberant daughter, I felt responsible for everyone's sadness. I was grateful when Wilf's mother, a nurse, offered to stay with Rachel and encouraged me to go home for a brief rest.

When I arrived home, Susie and her sister were there, busily cleaning. They had borrowed a ladder and climbed into the house through a second-story window. All the laundry lay neatly folded, and the house was immaculate. The orderliness helped calm me.

That the accident had happened under our mutual care reinforced the bond between Susie and me. We ached for each other. I was grateful for her presence.

I was relieved that Grace, a close friend and neighbor, had volunteered to take care of Phillip. We were fortunate to be a part of a caring neighborhood.

The sisters continued working while I sat down at the

kitchen table with an English muffin and tea. The events of the day swirled through my mind. *How long?* I kept asking myself, *How long before we know?*

Just then the telephone rang. It was Wilf's mother, Mary, calling from the hospital. There was excitement in her voice. "Sandy, Rachel's eyes are open!"

"Susie," I shouted, "Rachel's eyes are open! She's going to be all right! I know she's going to be all right!" I quickly grabbed my keys and purse and ran out the door.

Arriving at the hospital, I ran up two flights of stairs, down the pediatric corridor, and into ICU. Mary, my mother-in-law, looked optimistic. "Her eyes are open! She's going to get better, Sandy!"

Yes, it was true; her eyes were wide open. But for a second, I was afraid—her eyes were staring and not parallel. Then I threw my arms around Mary and exclaimed, "Oh, Mom, she's going to make it! Six hours and she's already opened her eyes!"

Hearing the creak of the heavy door, I looked up to see our friend Phil Hinton, a surgeon. I had called Kathy, his wife, earlier. We had known Kathy and Phil during Wilf's internship days before our stay in Nigeria. Seeing Phil now brought me strength. He was a remarkably outgoing, confident, warm, and positive person. I introduced Mom. Phil put his right hand on my shoulder and, looking directly at me, said, "Sandy, Rachel is in God's hands. He loves her more than we do. I would like to pray with you and Mary."

We surrounded Rachel's bed as Phil prayed. "Lord, we know the universe is in your hands. You are sovereign and can command even the wind to obey you. Rachel also is in your care. You can heal her! We ask you to heal her completely." His prayer gave me tremendous hope. *Yes,* I told myself, *Rachel will be healed.* This was the first of Phil's frequent visits.

As Phil left, a gentle-mannered, attractive nurse came into the room. "Hello, I'm Lupe. You must be Rachel's mother."

"Yes, I'm Sandy, and this is my mother-in-law, Mary."

"Oh, you're Dr. Derksen's mother! He's a wonderful doctor—so good with children." Her face became solemn. "Now his own child is here. I'm so sorry." I nodded gratefully, sensing that she cared.

Wilf came. He walked toward Rachel's bed. "Rachel's eyes are open," Mary said confidently. My husband's pale face looked drained. He was silent as he looked intently at Rachel. Lupe's eyes followed Wilf's with pain.

"It *is* a good sign, isn't it, Wilf," I asked expectantly, "that she opened her eyes this soon?"

"Any improvement is a good sign. As you both know, the first 48 hours are crucial. But—it's going to be a long wait." Wilf looked troubled as he left the room to resume his hospital duties.

I stayed with Rachel until one in the morning. Mary stayed with me except when she took time for a brief rest. Wilf, good at practical details, had arranged a room for us to use whenever we needed it. When she returned, she suggested that I try to get some sleep too.

As I lay in bed, awake, wanting to be with Rachel, my thoughts drifted to Nigeria, where we felt a closeness to life and death. . . .

———————◆———————

As a nurse, I had helped bring life back into other children in crises. I recalled the African town, Garkida, and its general hospital. Five years before, after one year of marriage, Wilf and I had traveled to this Nigerian village for three years of medical service. Wilf had just completed his medical internship and was looking forward to a time of service and experience before working on his pediatric specialty. The hospital to which he was assigned had 100 beds, and Wilf would be its only doctor. I had just completed nurse's training and was eager to apply what I had learned in a foreign hospital setting. We were young, inexperienced, and eager to enter a different culture.

Soon after arriving, I received midwifery training from Malama Shatu, the local head midwife, a large, beautiful, warm woman who easily became my friend.

One particular day there was no time to consult her. I was alone on duty. A Nigerian woman came staggering into the delivery area unannounced, obviously bent in pain and ready to give birth to her baby at any moment. Quickly I dashed toward her. Almost immediately, as I helped her onto the bed, the baby emerged. "Shi ne bomboi (It's a boy)," I announced. I noticed how tiny he was.

After clearing the airway with a bulb syringe, I saw that the baby was not breathing. I began resuscitation with quick motions. I felt for the heartbeat; it was faint and slow. "Ya mutu, ya mutu!" the mother screamed. ("He's dead, he's dead!")

Hot with fear, I moved the infant onto a higher table in a nearby room and continued resuscitation. Slowly the baby's color improved. He coughed and began to breathe.

It was absolutely musical, those wonderful baby sounds. "Thank you!" I whispered toward heaven. "Shi ne da rai (He's with life)," I told the mother as I wiped her wet forehead. She seemed afraid to believe.

Wilf came and reassured the mother that the child was fine. She dozed off, relieved and exhausted. Later she opened her eyes and reached with slender brown arms for her child. She smiled with weariness and joy. As droplets of perspiration still trickled down her tired but radiant face, she said in a whisper, "Na gode, Allah (Thank you, God)."

———◆———

This time it was my child who was in danger. What a luxury it would have been to begin the day again and enjoy Rachel climbing into my arms. But it was the middle of the night, and sleep wouldn't come. As I tossed restlessly, I searched my memories for hope. . . .

———◆———

Sometimes in Nigeria I would go through the wards of the Garkida General Hospital with Wilf in the evenings. Especially touching was the children's ward where mothers would feed their children or cool their hot bodies with wet towels. Night after night they seemed unaware of the hard floor as they lay on mats next to their children's beds, ready to attend to any need.

One boy's illness was especially difficult to witness. Yonana was about 12 but looked very old and lifeless. His face was haggard and sunken, his brown skin whitened and gray. His ribs and bones were pronounced, and fluid caused his abdomen to protrude, giving him the appearance of a severely malnourished child. He had advanced schistosomiasis, a parasitic disease with progressive liver damage.

Yonana suffered for two months, each day growing weaker and closer to death. Finally Wilf said there was nothing more he knew to do. We began to pray daily to God for him to intervene, to heal Yonana's body. Dale and Connie Nash, my sister and brother-in-law who had recently arrived, joined us in this effort. To our amazement, in a few weeks' time we saw Yonana regain complete health, something which had appeared medically impossible.

Some time later, the Nashes arrived at our home one evening for our weekly Bible study. Wilf told us all of a Nigerian woman who was very ill with peritonitis, an infection of the abdominal cavity. He feared she would likely die within 24 hours.

We remembered Yonana. Connie and I challenged our husbands to pray with this woman. When Wilf and Dale went to the hospital, they gathered the nurses together around her bed. Laying hands on the afflicted woman, they asked the creator of the universe to restore to health her infection-stricken body. The next day the woman's fever had subsided, and her condition improved. Subsequently she gained complete recovery.

On another occasion Wilf and Dale prayed for a child with cerebral malaria. Despite the use of appropriate medication, the boy was having persistent convulsions. Prayer was offered, and by the next day he was well.

———————◆———————

This time it was Rachel, our daughter. These memories gave me the hope I needed. Everything in me believed that she would be healed. I relaxed and was enveloped in sleep.

3

The Medical Prognosis

In the soft, early morning light, I washed my face. As I brushed my hair, a feeling of helplessness swept through me. *But,* I told myself, *I must be strong. Rachel will awaken.*

With confidence I walked quickly to ICU. Mary, gently stroking Rachel's hair, looked toward me as I entered the room. "Thanks for staying with Rachel, Mom. Oh, her eyes are closed."

"Yes, she closed them an hour ago."

"Any other changes?"

"No, it's been an uneventful night."

"Mom, Wilf and I are to meet with Dr. Dayton now. It won't be long. Then I'll stay with Rachel."

"That's fine, Sandy."

Wilf and I joined Dr. Dayton at the quiet end of the nurses' station. We listened attentively as he spoke.

"As you know, when Rachel arrived yesterday afternoon, her pupils were dilated and fixed. She had no heartbeat. From what you said, Sandy, you don't know how long she was under water—maybe 10 minutes, maybe 20?"

As I attempted to recall the events of the previous day, the image of Rachel at the side of the pool again flashed before me. For a long moment I could not speak. Finally I answered, "I—I just don't know—maybe 10 minutes. She had been next door playing inside with Kimberly before Kimberly went down the street to play with another friend, Tiffa—"

"But, Sandy," Wilf interrupted, "Susie told me that when Rachel came outside with her white purse, Kimberly had already gone to Tiffany's house. Rachel tried to open Susie's front door but was told to come back later because Jodi was sleeping. Susie saw Rachel walk to our front door. She finished watering, then went inside to the upstairs sewing room and cut out a dress before she looked out the window and saw Rachel in the pool."

"Wilf, I just assumed Rachel was safe, playing with Kimberly," I sobbed.

As Wilf took my trembling hand, Dr. Dayton gently continued the questions. "How long did it take for Rachel's color to improve?"

"She was purple and motionless when I found her. I thought she was already dead. I struggled for a second whether or not to even begin resuscitation. But I quickly grabbed her and started mouth-to-mouth breathing. Her color improved in about five minutes."

"Irreversible brain damage begins after five minutes. . . ." Dr. Dayton's words haunted my attempt to comprehend the rest of the discussion.

Dr. Dayton said that the first 24 hours were crucial and that if it took longer than 48 hours for Rachel to wake up, the outcome would begin to look grim. Then, if she survived, she would likely be a severely brain-damaged child.

"But," Wilf added, "children have been reported to have tolerated longer periods." He sounded hopeful.

"Yes, there are some good signs," Dr. Dayton continued. "Yesterday afternoon her pupils began to respond slightly." I looked intently at Wilf, then again focused my attention on Dr. Dayton. "At 6:00 P.M. she made a few gasping respirations, a sign she's fighting the respirator. In the evening she opened her eyes, began moving her tongue, and withdrawing from pain on the upper extremities. These are all favorable signs, but we still don't know her prognosis. Another EEG (electroencephalogram) needs to be done today and one tomorrow for comparison."

Dr. Dayton had been honest yet loving from the beginning when he had embraced Wilf in the emergency room and let him cry. Now he sat forward and put his hands firmly on each of us. "I do not believe in camouflaging the facts, but you know I share your faith in God. I will continue to pray for you and to do everything within my power medically to help."

The facts were hard to assimilate, but I knew, regardless

of the medical data, God could and would heal our daughter.

On my way down the corridor after leaving Wilf and Dr. Dayton, I met Mary. I hugged her good-bye and thanked her for coming. She said she would be back later that day.

As I walked into ICU, a nurse was just finishing Rachel's bath. She said good morning as she carried the washbasin and towel to the sink. After emptying the basin, she walked out the door, saying she'd be back in a few minutes.

Sitting beside the bed, I began talking to Rachel quietly. As I stroked her face, her eyes began to open. Standing up, I leaned over the bed and said, "Rachel, Mommy's here; can you hear me talking to you?"

Rachel's eyes began to focus, her arms reached forward slightly, and a frightened look came over her face. "Rachel, Mommy's here. You're going to be all right." I leaned over her bed to hold her. As I did so, her arms returned to a motionless position on the bed; her eyes became a blank stare again.

I wanted to tell someone, but perhaps I had imagined it. *What proof did I have that Rachel had responded to me?* But I knew it was real, and I was filled with hope. *If she did it once, then she will do it again. But what about the frightened look? What did she see? What was she thinking? Did she see Jesus and heaven?* My mind was full of questions. *Maybe she did not want to return to this life. Where was her spirit the day before when her heart had stopped beating?* I looked down upon Rachel's motionless body and wondered: *Is she really here, or has she begun another journey? Where is Rachel now?*

Wilf walked in then and told me that he would be meeting my parents around noon at the Fresno Airport. He looked at Rachel with a characteristic wrinkle in his brow, like Rachel's when she was pensive. I knew it was painful for him to see her staring blankly.

"Wilf," I began hesitantly. "Rachel focused her eyes and looked directly at mine. Her arms reached toward me. It only lasted a few seconds, but I know it was a definite response."

"Well, Sandy," he was gentle in his tone, "often when there has been brain damage, the face can twitch or the arms might jerk involuntarily."

"But, Wilf, this was different! She had a frightened look on her face—a real expression!"

Wilf just stared at Rachel silently. He gently touched my shoulder. "Sandy, I'm going now to meet your parents."

I nodded. I felt a great responsibility for Wilf's pain. I wanted to tell him I was sure Rachel would be all right, but I did not know how to adequately express my conviction to him.

4

Circle of Love

While walking in the hospital hall, I heard a familiar voice behind me. I turned to see Grace. We embraced. "How's Phillip?" I asked.

"Spunky, fun, normal—" We both felt awkward at the word *normal*. "Oh, Sandy, why did this have to happen to you—to Rachel? It's—it's not right!" I loved Grace for being herself, for her empathy. "Sandy, I'd like to see Rachel."

Just then Lupe motioned to me. "Go on in, Grace," I said, pointing toward the direction of the room. "I'll be there soon." I walked to the nurses' station.

Lupe seemed concerned. "Sandy, Dr. Dayton plans to look in on Rachel soon."

"Thanks, Lupe, I'll be in her room."

As I turned down the corridor, Grace was walking toward me sobbing. Reaching her, I put my arms around her shoulders.

"I'm sorry, Sandy, I didn't want to cry. It's—I feel horrible seeing Rachel like that!"

"Grace," I said confidently, "she's in God's hands." But for an instant I questioned my words. *Was I so sure Rachel would live? What if she died? Would I leave her in God's hands then?* I quickly pushed this thought aside. *I must be strong!*

Grace and I held each other close. Her tears were a comfort to me because I knew she cared. I remembered the intimate talks we'd had. I thought of all our laughing and crying, of feeling safe enough to speak honestly and learning how to do it in love.

While Grace was with me, my parents arrived. I watched them as they looked at Rachel. Tears welled up in my mother's eyes. She spoke soft, loving words to a motionless Rachel as if she were listening.

Just last month I had taken Phillip and Rachel to my parents' home. Each morning Rachel had awakened them with hugs and kisses. I recalled her chasing butterflies in Mom's flower garden. Now as Mom and I embraced, tears flowed quietly down our cheeks. Few words were spoken. Mom went with Grace to get Phillip. Dad stayed at the hospital with me. His composure and love were reassuring.

That evening was a blur of faces, embraces, tubes, and uniforms in and out of Rachel's room. Wilf came to see Rachel whenever possible while continuing his usual medical duties in the hospital. Tenaciously I hung onto hope. Wilf's calmness was a comfort to me.

The following morning, the third day since the accident, a number of friends arrived at the hospital simultaneously. Many of these friends were members of our congregation. Wilf gathered them together in a room to pray, also asking Dr. Dayton to come. Each had experienced personal suffering in the form of serious illnesses or handicapped children.

Mike Dayton began by saying, "Let me briefly explain that there have been some positive signs in Rachel's condition, but not enough yet. We still don't know her prognosis. Let's submit our helplessness to God."

We felt a deep bond of quiet empathy as each in turn prayed for Rachel.

On the fourth day we had a conference with the neurologist. "The EEG shows no improvement. The brain continues to swell. Another EEG will be taken tomorrow to see if there is any change." His expression gave no encouragement.

"The signs are not promising." Mike Dayton's voice was steady. "The spasticity and posturing, the abnormal muscle stretching, and the arm contractions decrease our hope."

"Are you saying that her prognosis is not good?" Wilf asked stiffly, knowing the answer.

"Yes," the neurologist answered. Mike nodded his head in agreement.

Still I went away with new determination that Rachel would be well. If God was healing her, and I continued to believe he was, the facts did not matter.

I must praise God for what he is doing and thank him for this situation, I told myself. *I cannot let my feelings change my thinking about God's intention to heal. But what do I do with the twinges of doubt, those waves of questioning? If I let myself feel, then I become afraid. Thoughts of her never recovering begin to surface. If I doubt God, he may not heal her. Some say I must keep thanking and praising God. But how can I thank and praise God? I must stop these emotions. I must keep believing!*

That afternoon the door to Rachel's room opened slowly. It was Susie. Hesitantly she asked, "May I come in?" I motioned for her to sit on the chair beside me.

"Sandy, I've been wanting to come, but I've been scared. Is there any change?"

"No, Susie, she's about the same. How are your girls?"

"Kimberly keeps asking about Rachel and wants to come see her."

"When I was home yesterday, Susie, I saw Kimberly on the porch. She asked me if Rachel still looked blue. It must be upsetting for her to maintain that impression as her last memory of Rachel. Perhaps if she saw Rachel now, she would have a better image of her."

"Maybe so—look! Rachel's opening her eyes!" Susie exclaimed, leaning over the bed.

"Yes, she opens and closes them, but she just stares blankly. She's not aware, I'm told."

"Are you sure, Sandy? It seems like she hears us talking."

"I talk to her as if she does," I replied.

"She's going to make it, isn't she, Sandy?"

"Yes, Susie, I'm sure she will."

"She must be listening!" Susie was adamant. "Rachel! You're going to be all right. We love you. Kimberly wants to play with you. Jodi misses you too." Susie caressed Rachel's still hand while tears fell down her face.

"Susie, Rachel loves being at your place. She's crazy about Kimberly. They get along so well."

"Jim and I are amazed to hear Rachel sing on key. One evening at our house she sang 'Jesus Loves Me' at the top of her voice. She talks continuously and so clearly. It makes one believe she is older than three."

"Someday they will play again," I assured Susie. Silently I prayed, *Oh, God, please make it happen soon!*

"Sandy, I love her like one of my own daughters."

"I know, Susie."

Rachel continued to lie still and seemingly lifeless. A nurse came in. I left the hospital with Susie to go home for supper.

The following Sunday Wilf was working. I asked Phil and Kathy Hinton to pick me up to go to the Sunday evening meeting at their church, a church that emphasized the power of the Spirit in the Christian's life. I felt a deep need for the support of other Christians who believed in miraculous healing.

I walked in with Phil and Kathy, full of anticipation. Phil led us to the front row. I felt warmth and love as I sat down even though I didn't know the other people. I cannot remember much about the message, but after the service, Roger, the pastor, said the elders and ministers would be available to pray with those who had needs. I felt a strong urge to go to the front.

I began to relate my needs to an assistant pastor. He told me the church had been praying for Rachel. Pastor Roger had gone with Phil to pray for her several times. I was so appreciative of these people's care and belief. As he prayed with me, tears of gratitude flowed easily. I left, filled with renewed hope.

That night, while lying in bed, I remembered the unique occasion of Rachel's birth. "Daughter of Garkida" the village affectionately called her. She was the first white child birthed at the Garkida Hospital Obstetrical Ward.

———◆———

"Wilf! Wake up! I'm having a contraction. Do you think it's for real?"

Wilf finally opened his eyes, but by then the contraction was over. "Let me in on the next one," he mumbled, as he stuffed the pillow back under his head. Soon he was breathing deeply again.

Maybe the baby will be crazy like Wilf, I thought. Lying flat on my back, wide awake and nervous, I kept telling myself how fortunate I was to be with a doctor, even if he was asleep.

The night was quiet—there was no distant drumming, no dogs howling. Even the fruit bats and the owls were silent. Only the wind rippled gently through the nem trees, enhancing the peace. But I could hear every leaf quiver. It seemed each inch of my body and soul was alive.

In Africa! Is my baby truly to be born in Africa? Tonight? Wilf, how can you sleep? This might be the happiest night of our lives together. I wondered and dreamed and was glad and scared all over again. The questions whirled in the wind of my mind while the air outside played with the leaves.

I imagined ways I would tell our child some day of the great continent of Africa, of the strange beauty and immense contrast, and especially of Garkida, this village we had grown to love.

"Wilf, it's back again!"

This time Wilf shot into a sitting position and put his hand on my abdomen. "Sandy, it's for real!"

"You don't have to tell me that!"

Between contractions we talked with quiet excitement. Then Wilf untucked the mosquito net, got out of bed, and told me he was going to gather together the camera and tape player with which he planned to record some of the delivery events. Soon I could hear him taking a bath in the adjoining room. He was singing "It's a Long, Long Road to Freedom." I joined in the singing as I stepped out of bed and rechecked the bag I had prepared. Then I listened with amusement as Wilf talked enthusiastically to himself. "Yes, sir! This is going to be a first! No doubt about that!" Then he called out, "Sandy? How do you feel? Any more movement?"

"Yes, plenty!" I laughed and looked up at Wilf, who

had emerged from the bathroom. "Wilf, I feel so energetic! Want to play tennis?"

Laughingly he replied, "It's too dark, otherwise I'd take you up on it."

"Excuses, excuses—"

Wilf fixed some breakfast and we ate, then we just sat there, sharing a quiet, eager joy. When Wilf suggested perhaps we should go to the hospital, I was more than willing. We descended the hill slowly, arm in arm, tripping now and again over a small twig or rock. As we walked, Wilf exclaimed, "Sandy, we're unique! We not only produce babies, we know how to deliver them." I smiled half-heartedly as another contraction began. I'd be oh, so glad to crawl into a bed.

We had both agreed that Shatu should be the midwife in charge of this birth. She had been pleased as it would be the first time she would deliver a white baby. As we entered the hospital's maternity ward, Wilf greeted her, "Sanu, Malama Shatu! Lafia? (Hello! How are you?)"

"Lafia (Fine)," she answered. A large, welcoming smile lit her beautiful face. "Sanu, Sandy, so the time has come."

I was happy to be taken care of by my teacher, friend, and now charge midwife. Wilf knew I was in good hands, and soon he returned home to prepare himself for a full day of medical work ahead. His confidence gave me much assurance.

For the remainder of the night, I dozed sporadically, damp with the physical work of labor. Kind Shatu stayed close, offering words of encouragement. By dawn

37

the contractions were coming much closer together. Finally there was only the space of a few minutes between them.

Listening to the gentle sounds of mothers talking to their babies and to each other gave me strength to persevere, but it was difficult, for the contractions were becoming stronger and stronger. Now the labor multiplied with every strained breath. Wilf had returned to be with me, and I grabbed his wrist tightly. There was almost no time to breathe between contractions, and with each one the discomfort intensified. Wilf encouraged me to breathe rhythmically.

"Wilf, I have to quit. I can't do this much longer!"

"I'm afraid we got ourselves into this and you've got to go through with it now."

"It will be over soon." Shatu's voice was reassuring.

Suddenly I became the center of attention. I rather liked it—this being on stage. The novelty overcame the misery. I wanted to show these Nigerian friends that I, a white woman, could have a baby as naturally as they did. The nurses' excitement was intense and energizing. They were waiting to see, for the first time, a white baby's birth. "Sanu, Sandy, sorry, sorry, Sandy." Mwapu; slender, smiling Rahila; a student from another village; and Kucheli, who had so recently been through this—all these young midwives took turns wiping the dampness from my forehead or rubbing my legs to lessen the cramping. What beautiful faces—what beautiful, caring faces! I suddenly realized, even amid my great discomfort, how deeply I loved these Nigerian friends.

I looked for Wilf and found his serious blue eyes. *He will be a good father,* I thought. While I continued gazing into his eyes, he reached for my hand, giving me strength. "Sandy, I'm so proud of you," he whispered.

I looked past Wilf and saw Mary Dadisman, an American nurse who had lived in Garkida for many years. In addition to the midwifery instruction I had received from Shatu, Mary also had given me many tips. Now she stood among these friends, encouraging me.

"I'll try five minutes longer, and then I'll have to quit," I announced firmly. Everyone laughed, but my guess was correct. I gave the final push. Suddenly there was a lusty cry—a serious infant cry—the first sound of life.

"It's a girl!" Wilf shouted jubilantly. "It's 12:40, Wednesday, October 24."

"Rachel Ann Derksen," I announced.

Shatu held the wiggling one and brought her to me. She was beautiful and perfect. Her eyes were already wide open; she had thick black hair and long fingernails.

There was nothing in my past with which to relate my emotions, this ecstatic yet peaceful knowledge that I was, for the first time in my life, a mother. There was an excited mixture of Bura, Hausa, and English in the room. No one had any difficulty communicating. Everyone was laughing, touching a common gladness.

———————◆———————

I thought for a long time on this miracle. The following morning I walked down the familiar corridor to Rachel's room, expecting her to sit and speak to me as I entered. Of course she did not. I wanted to command her, as Jesus did the little girl he healed: "Get up, my child, and walk!" I wanted to gather together everything within me, all of my hope and faith and mental energy, and call down angels and heavenly powers and shout, "Rachel, in Jesus' name, arise and be made whole!" But the words wouldn't come.

5

Friends

A week had passed since Rachel's accident. I was afraid to share my deepest thoughts. *God will heal Rachel,* I continued to reassure myself. The expressions on people's faces were not offering hope any longer. I began to have doubts, but I still wanted to believe. My stomach was in knots.

The recent past had been a time of growth for me. I had learned to better understand myself as well as the nature of my relationships with my friends, my children, and particularly with Wilf. Wilf's busy residency immediately after our return from Nigeria had left me with the responsibility of rearing two small children essentially alone. We had decided to move closer to the hospital to allow Wilf more time with the family.

Several of Wilf's long-time friends plus members of his

family came to help us on the day of the move. By the middle of the evening we had hauled all our furniture and belongings into our new home. By that time I was physically exhausted but felt happy as we chatted on our front porch, eating a much-deserved supper. I knew Wilf's schedule at the hospital would still be demanding, but at least the close proximity would allow us to share more time together as a family.

We discovered that 20 to 25 people met weekly at one of the homes in the neighborhood for potluck dinners. I became acquainted with our new neighbors in this way, but it was difficult to have more than superficial conversation while around us were young children requiring supervision. Everyone was friendly, and those who knew Wilf were especially glad to have us in the neighborhood. Many had attended college and church with him in the past.

I loved the house and would lie in bed at night with visions of decorating possibilities running through my mind. The visions took a long time to actualize, however, with many belongings to put away and two little people to watch constantly.

I began planning for Christmas and invited my family to spend the holiday with us. Just before the date of their arrival, our neighborhood arranged a housewarming for us. Each family that came brought a decoration for our Christmas tree. The house was filled with children and laughter. Gary, who lived across the street, gave a short welcoming speech, then we all sang Christmas carols. It was a wonderful and memorable occasion.

But the Christmas festivities passed, and life was soon back to its normal daily routine. I found myself becoming increasingly depressed. I enjoyed our home and our family, but I longed for Wilf to be more a part of it.

Was this all there was to family life? I asked myself. *Do other medical wives share this same loneliness? Where had all my dreams gone?*

I wanted to be an excellent wife and mother, but my fantasy was being shattered. I was losing my enthusiasm to clean the house and enjoy the time when Wilf was at home. I found myself being impatient with the children. The joy of living slowly vanished.

Sensing I was unhappy, a close relative tried to help in his gentle way by pointing out all my blessings: a good husband, two beautiful, healthy children, a comfortable home, a friendly neighborhood. He was right—there was no reason to be miserable. *I should not feel this way,* I thought. I tried to smile and push away the negative feelings which persisted. After calling a few doctors' wives to see if any could identify with my situation, I felt even worse. None seemed to understand, and I felt terribly alone.

One afternoon a friend called, sincerely wanting to know how I was doing. Through my tears, I told her how miserable I felt. She suggested I talk to a friend of hers who was a counselor. So, a few days later, I went to Myron Downing's office. People called him "Doc" because of his M.D. initials.

I did not know how to begin but was put at ease immediately. I felt accepted and began to pour out my frustrations. For the first time in months I felt as if someone understood. This was the beginning of learning to know myself better.

I became aware that I had allowed disappointments and resentments to accumulate. Many of these feelings and expectations had begun in Nigeria early in our marriage. Certainly I wanted Wilf to be a conscientious doctor, but his hospital work consumed our personal time as husband and wife. I felt guilty when I complained about his preoccupation with his work, but I yearned for uninterrupted moments to share with him my inner thoughts and the events of each day. My needs seemed to shrink in importance, however, when Wilf was concerned with how to help save a child's life or how to approach a difficult surgery, so I kept my thoughts to myself much of the time.

Eventually I became less dependent on Wilf as I began to teach English to nursing students and started a preschool of about 20 children. Later I became involved with delivering babies in order to help with some of the evening maternity work load. It was a fulfilling life. Getting to know many of the Nigerian women, sharing meals, learning crafts from one another, and times with the other Americans kept life interesting. Circumstances, however, did not allow our marriage relationship to be all that I had dreamed it would be.

As I talked with Doc, I realized it was possible to have two or more competing feelings at one time. For example, I wanted to be in Nigeria, and I encouraged Wilf to work in whatever way he was needed. However, I did not like what it was doing to our relationship, to the communication between us. But I put off doing anything about the problem by saying to myself that the frustration would pass when we returned to California.

What I did not know was that he would be just as busy in California, and his work would not be nearly as fulfilling. After being his own boss in Nigeria for three years, going into a residency program—in a sense becoming a student again—was a difficult adjustment for him. He had his own difficulties to face.

Even though I had looked forward to returning to California because of my hope for a more satisfying personal situation, I was ill prepared for adjusting back into American life. Caring for Rachel in Garkida had been natural and simple; here it seemed more complicated. She was not as content. I wanted Wilf to be more involved in her nurturing, but he was too busy! Nor was it easy when Phillip was born. For the first few months of his life he was a very fussy baby, and Rachel, who was still quite young, also required much attention.

I wanted to be an ideal wife and mother, but I felt I was failing. Doc helped me see all the "shoulds" I had set up for myself and the unproductive guilt this had produced. As we talked, it became clear I had set up rather unrealistic expectations for myself.

I continued to see Doc a few more times. Learning to accept my emotions and not to classify them as right or wrong helped me become more honest with myself and with Wilf. Like many other Christians, I experienced much guilt whenever I was angry or lonely and unable to maintain a constant level of happy feelings. Doc suggested ways

I could find release from self-punishment as he talked with me about the variety of personalities in the Bible and the many emotions each of them communicated. He mentioned spiritual concepts which worked in practical ways to deal with guilt and anger, like "speaking the truth in love" and "not letting the sun go down on one's wrath."

I discovered I had been lying to myself about my anger. I could not manufacture good feelings by denying my angry ones; I could only feel the way I felt. Failing at times was inevitable. I needed to recognize and acknowledge my feelings and then decide how best to share them.

Trying hard to do everything well and not always succeeding made me feel I did nothing well. Without knowing it, I had begun to resent my role as a mother. As I realized this, I began to accept myself and my circumstances, changing what I could. I became less dependent on Wilf for my fulfillment; I recognized it was not solely *his* responsibility to make me happy. Our communication became much more open and our limited time together with the children increased in quality and joy.

At a neighborhood coffee time, I told the women of my past depression, my visits with Doc, and how inner healing was taking place at home. This was the beginning of a share-group composed of eight women, including me, with Doc as our leader. The group was still meeting when Rachel's accident occurred. I was thankful for their support and knew I could depend on them for encouragement as we waited for our beautiful Rachel to awaken.

One day, in passing, I saw Susie. I let her know my plan to attend the next group meeting and encouraged her to be a part of it. She seemed uneasy about going but said she might do so.

As I thought about the sessions of the last five months, I remembered the growing acceptance and understanding we had experienced of ourselves as well as of one another. It was worthwhile, this "being transparent," despite the occasional tensions that developed. Doc was a good leader, a nonthreatening person who had helped us learn to understand the nature of our feelings better and the positive ways in which we could use even the most uncomfortable ones. While it would not be easy, I was eagerly anticipating the next meeting.

Nine days had passed since Rachel's accident. Still many of the women in our group did not know the sequence of events that led up to it. As I arrived for our group session, other women were already there and settling down with their coffee or tea. I saw Susie and sensed her uneasiness. After greeting her and the other women, I sat down. I was aware of the tension in the room, and I knew they were waiting for me to begin.

I reviewed Rachel's condition calmly, sharing that there was not much improvement but that I was still hopeful. Then I told them briefly about the accident, concerned that they should accurately know what had happened so that blame would not be placed on myself or Susie. Fears constantly battered my mind. Would people regard me as negligent? I wanted them to realize I was not—and neither was Susie.

Doc suggested that each woman share how she was feeling about Susie and me. As they did so, the blame seemed turned more toward Susie, perhaps because they wanted to relieve whatever guilt I might be feeling. I did not want this to happen. Susie was one of my closest friends. She knew and loved Rachel almost as her own. Our friendship had become very intimate during the last six months.

A realization of how much pain Susie recently had suffered became vivid. Less than nine months before, her sister had died unexpectedly during pregnancy. On her deathbed, she had asked Susie to adopt her four-year-old son. Even though Susie had promised to adopt him, she was not immediately able to do so. When she and her husband did pursue the adoption, for unexplained reasons the court would not allow it. Susie felt guilt and remorse for the promise she had been unable to keep. Now for Susie to receive the greater share of blame for Rachel's accident was not fair. She was not responsible. I did not want the women to think it was her fault, so I began to tell in detail the circumstances of the accident. Susie gave her perspective and wept as she expressed the misery she felt because of Rachel's tragedy.

The group identified with us as mothers. They told of incidents that had happened to them. They admitted that accidents happen all the time, but usually not with such devastating results. We all agreed we could not protect our children 24 hours a day, nor would it be healthy to try.

The issue of blame became secondary to concern for Susie, me, and Rachel. Doc helped us all to realize how our own fears and guilt frequently cause us to interpret another's behavior with judgment and criticism. I left my friends that day feeling a burden had been lifted. I sensed warm acceptance and felt "safe," and I eagerly anticipated our next time together.

6

I Can't

"She looks so peaceful, doesn't she, Lupe?" Rachel's eyes were closed as if she were in a deep sleep.

"Yes, she does, Sandy. Her color is better today."

"Rachel will wake up soon, Lupe; I know God will heal her."

"Maybe—I keep praying, Sandy."

"Thank you, Lupe. You are so good to her! All the doctors and nurses are so kind to Rachel and to us."

After Lupe had gone for lunch, I quietly let down Rachel's bed rail and sat close to her. As I began to stroke her arm, I felt a calm. Ten days had passed since the accident. Recently I had read and heard many scripture passages which reassured me of God's ability to heal, to perform any miracle. I knew God was asking me to wait on him, that he knew when to heal her. Perhaps many people would see or hear of Rachel's miracle and come to believe in Jesus. Then her horrible drowning would be redeemed.

"I love you, Rachel," I spoke to her softly. "Jesus loves you. The mornings aren't the same without hearing you say, 'Let's get up!' Even in Nigeria you were an early riser. We would hear your baby noises, and Daddy would bring you to our bed. The months after your birth were cool ones, so he would wrap you in your own special blanket, and we would move to sit in front of the fireplace. Snuggled inside my robe, you would nurse. Your tiny fingers touched and squeezed my soft robe as your enormous blue eyes focused on me.

"Daddy sat near us, reading. We listened to the sounds of the village awakening—the chickens crowing and people busy with their morning activities.

"I still recall the first time we walked to the market. You were only three months old. A friend, Salinah, encouraged me to carry you on my back as she carried her baby, Nehemiah. We wrapped one cloth to support you from the bottom and another to hold your neck and shoulders straight. That was the beginning of learning the Nigerian way.

"We took walks around the village, visiting friends. We would take rides on the back of Daddy's motorcycle with Daji, our funny little dog, crouching on the handlebars. The people would laugh and shout greetings as we went by! The village mothers were proud that I carried you as they carried their own. Many loved you, Rachel. Many love you now."

My words to Rachel were interrupted as Janet, Wilf's sister, walked in with a friend to stay with Rachel for a few hours. I took this opportunity to go home.

Wilf and I were grateful that my parents did all they could to keep our home running as normally as possible. When I arrived home, Mother warmed soup for me as I asked about Phillip. "He and his grandpa have had a great time outdoors working in the garden and playing ball," she replied.

When I opened the back door, Phillip saw me and came running as fast as his stubby little legs would let him. At first glance, he looked like Rachel. I lifted him and held him close. The warmth of his body was comforting. He rested his head on my shoulder as I walked into the kitchen. He would soon be ready for a nap, but I wanted him with me for a while.

After romping and playing together in the living room, I brought out some quiet playthings for Phillip. Seeing the fireplace in front of me, I remembered a family time several months ago, long before this terrible event.

———————◆———————

The four of us were lounging in the living room. "It's nice to just sit here and listen to the rain," I remarked to Wilf.

"Yes, it is. I'll build a fire, Sandy, if you'll put Phillip to bed. It's a perfect evening to sit in front of the fireplace."

"Sounds great to me!" I picked up seven-month-old

Phillip who was playing on the living room rug and motioned to Rachel. "Come, let's get your pajamas on too."

"I don't want to go to bed!" Rachel stated loudly.

"You can go to bed later, but just put your pajamas on now."

"Oh, all right. Phillip's going to bed?"

"Yes, Rachel, he's very tired." I carried Phillip upstairs with Rachel walking up beside us. In a few minutes Phillip was content in bed, and Rachel had struggled successfully to put on her own nightclothes.

"Now let's go downstairs," Rachel said bossily as she looked up at me. Walking downstairs, we heard the sounds of a Beethoven sonata which Wilf was playing on our piano with his usual absorption.

"Daddy made a fire!" Rachel called exuberantly from the living room. She began skipping and jumping, first on the living room rug and then through the adjoining rooms, concluding her energetic dance by climbing onto Wilf's knees just as he was finishing the last movement of the sonata with a grand flourish. He paused long enough to give Rachel a smile and hug, then began an elaborate improvisation of our daughter's favorite song, "Jesus Loves Me." Rachel chimed in enthusiastically, improvising a bit herself.

The three of us settled in front of the crackling fire to enjoy each other and Wilf's favorite snack—peanuts and oranges.

"Man, it's good to play the piano! I sure don't get enough time these days."

"I love your music, Wilf."

"Hear that noise?" Rachel piped in. "Listen! What is it? The fire poppin'?"

"That's right." Wilf began cracking peanuts for Rachel.

"Daddy, let me do it myself! I know how!"

I was thankful Rachel had such determination, but at times it was exhausting.

Quiet, unrushed evenings were still unusual for us, although not so rare as they once had been. As we talked, Rachel listened and added her own opinions and elaborations every now and then. When she began to yawn, Wilf reached for a nearby storybook. As Rachel sat on his lap, he read, "Tommy brushed his teeth and combed his hair—all by himself because Tommy's a big boy now."

"I'm big too! I'm not a boy. I'm a girl. I have a big tummy too!" I smiled. Rachel loved to end her sentences with *too*.

"Yes, you certainly do have a big tummy!" Wilf agreed as he pulled Rachel's pajama shirt up to look at it. As he tickled it, she giggled with delight, then asked Daddy to finish the story. Later, Wilf carried her to bed.

I soon followed them. I was filled with a deep love as I bent down to kiss our first child. "What a perfect family," I said softly. "God has given us so much."

———◆———

Now, with Rachel in the hospital, our family life was markedly incomplete.

The next morning I walked into Rachel's room and

noticed that she appeared more withdrawn from life. Her coloring was very pale. Later, at midmorning, I heard a commotion in ICU. By Rachel's bed stood a doctor and two nurses. After questioning them, I realized a tube had slipped too deeply into her lungs. Not wanting human mistakes to upset Rachel's healing process, I became very angry and spoke words to the doctor I later regretted.

The doctor and nurses continued trying to correct whatever had gone wrong with the tube. Sensing I should stay out of their way, I walked down the hall. Needing someone to talk to, I went toward the nearest phone. As I began to dial, disappointment and anger brought tears to my eyes. I was calling Wilf's sister Janet, but when she answered, I could barely speak. "Rachel looks awful," I told her, "and something went wrong with the tube to her lungs."

Janet listened, then gently said, "Sandy, we all want her to be healed, but have you thought of the possibility that she may not get better? Are you willing to let her go and give her back to God?"

I was stunned. I had surrounded myself with people who had prayed for Rachel's healing with confidence that God would perform a miracle. That was what I wanted to hear. Now someone very close to me was asking me to search my heart and consider giving our precious gift back to God.

"Janet, I can't! I want her healed! I want her back the way she was!" Sobbing, I walked into Rachel's room. Looking at Rachel, I said, "I can't give her back! I want her! Lupe, do I have to let her go?"

"Yes, Sandy, you do." She put her arm around me. We wept together.

7

Letting Go

No, I won't let her go! my mind screamed. Looking around, I saw sad, worried faces. The room was full of restless energy. Someone would go for coffee or tea, another moved from a chair to the floor. The air was filled with the nervous buzz of women trying to make conversation.

It seemed like months since I had last been to the share-group, yet it had been less than a week. I was confused and lonely. Rachel had been in the hospital now for two weeks, and she was still comatose.

Everyone looked my way. I began talking, sounding less shaky than I felt. "Rachel is not getting any better. None of the doctors believes she will." Hearing myself say these words was frightening. "If she does, she will be severely brain damaged." Still afraid but wanting to be hopeful, I continued, "I know God can still perform a miracle."

But my emotions screamed inside of me, and I could contain them no longer. I blurted out, "I can't let Rachel die! Am I the only one who believes? Have you given up just like the others? Does anyone believe in miracles anymore?"

The silence thundered; nobody moved. The pale faces flinched. No one could find words. Finally I was beginning to crash under the weight of the huge burden I had been confidently trying to carry alone. The tears spilled out, and I covered my eyes with my hands. Doc, who had been sitting on the floor across the room from me, moved beside the couch where I was sitting and put his hand on my arm.

I heard my name. It was Grace, and her voice was shaking. "Sandy—I believe in miracles—" Her words sounded dubious, but I knew she meant them or at least wanted to mean them.

Then I began questioning myself. *Do I still believe in miracles?* Now my words spilled out uncensored without piety or justification. "I don't want her back abnormal! I want her the way she was, beautiful and bright. I want the Rachel I know! Don't any of my prayers matter? Doesn't God hear anymore?"

Most of the women were crying. I looked at Susie, Grace, and Doc. Tears streamed down their faces. Then everybody wanted to talk at once. They all spoke from deep within of their own fears as well as of their concerns for me.

"I was angry and upset," Grace said, "the first time I saw Rachel in the hospital with all those wires and tubes connected to her small body. She seemed so violated."

Now Grace was speaking more easily. "I was startled when she opened her eyes. They were not parallel—those big, beautiful eyes. After seeing Rachel, I felt the need to go home to see Jed, my own son. When I got there, I looked at Jed, who was sound asleep. He was a picture of health. I shook him gently, wanting him to open his eyes. I was relieved to see that they were parallel. It was strange that I felt compelled to see his eyes. I stood by his bed a long time and prayed. I was so thankful for Jed, that he was healthy.

"But in contrast to Rachel's condition, it was unfair. At first I tried to keep Jed away from you, Sandy. When you told me it was good to see him, I relaxed. You even took time to be with my boys. That meant a lot."

Someone spoke from across the room. "I'm afraid to let John out of my sight—afraid something might happen to my child. It's difficult to be carefree and natural anymore."

"Why did it have to be Rachel?" I blurted out angrily.

"She was perfect!" another member sobbed. Her own child had recently suffered a serious illness but had survived. Just knowing that someone else had experienced similar feelings helped.

Susie exploded with, "Sandy, she has to live! God, you can't let her die! No matter how she comes back to us, we must have her back!" She was sitting huddled on the floor as she sobbed these words. Her face was drawn with fear and anger. I felt very close to my friend. Someone reached over to touch her. She continued, "I love her too much to let her go, even if she's different now."

I looked at Susie. "For a long time I have been strong," I said. "I believed God would heal Rachel. I don't understand his ways, and now it is difficult to trust him. But who else can I go to? I don't understand, but I do know that I need to be willing to release her. I need to give Rachel back to—to God." The words almost caught in my throat. "Maybe he will still intervene and give her back to me. I'm—I'm going to leave her in his hands." I sobbed quietly, feeling insignificant and helpless. The room was still.

Doc motioned for Susie and me to stand, gently leading us to the middle of the room. Everyone encircled us. We stood there silently for a few moments, experiencing the love and support of the group as never before.

Doc said, "Let's pray." I sensed the nearness of the Holy Spirit and the closeness of our spirits one with another. We all felt a profound unity and closeness as we each offered a short prayer. There was much strength and peace in the room. Afterward each person hugged me.

When Grace and I embraced, she said, "This is the closest I've ever felt toward any woman in the group. Being so close to you has made me feel as if I could touch God."

Susie and I embraced and clung to each other. The bond between us was renewed and stronger than ever, yet I knew there was a difficult road ahead.

8

The Decision

Dr. Dayton began, "Wilf and Sandy, as you know, Rachel's prognosis is very poor. The other doctors and I have discussed Rachel's physical condition. We want you to think about the possibilities concerning her care. We have read the EEGs and noted the abnormal neurological signs—"

I looked at Wilf. His face was intent.

"Hope of any functional recovery is minimal if at all," added the neurologist.

"Do you mean she could live on indefinitely as she is now?" I asked.

"Yes. That is the reason we think it best to give only minimal supportive care."

I knew this would mean taking her off the respirator

and not doing cardiopulmonary resuscitation if she stopped breathing.

Dr. Granoff spoke. "It is necessary that we transfer her out of ICU into a private room."

At this point there was a short discussion among the doctors. There was some hesitancy about doing this immediately. Their conversation sounded cold. I realized it was necessary to use basic, precise medical terminology to clarify the issues, but it all seemed very impersonal. They were talking about our daughter, our little girl who had played, laughed, and cried just less than three weeks before. Now she was comatose, and we had to decide where to "put" her and what or what not to "put into" her. Or perhaps we were not talking about Rachel at all but only her body. I could not fault the doctors for only doing their job; I was glad they were thorough, and I knew they cared. I just wished I did not have to listen to the medical facts, and that I didn't understand them so well.

"We need to know if you want Rachel on the respirator indefinitely. If we continue using it, then a tracheotomy should be done. Otherwise we will remove the respirator." Dr. Granoff came right to the point. He was firm, but his voice carried kindness.

Wilf had been quiet, and I knew he had been carefully analyzing and weighing the situation. "We understand. Sandy and I will need time to discuss the possibilities," he said, his voice heavy with fatigue.

The doctors all reassured us that they would support whatever decision we made. There was nothing left to discuss. We stood and said good-bye. The doctors looked vulnerable and helplessly human. I knew they wished they could heal Rachel.

Wilf and I made our way down the stairs to the hospital cafeteria. We sat across from each other, Wilf with his coffee and me with my orange juice, oblivious to the people around us.

"Wilf, would they just suddenly take away the respirator?"

"No, Rachel would be weaned from it slowly."

That sounded better—less abrupt than I had first thought. Struggling to express myself, I finally blurted, "Wilf, I'm ready to let her go if that's what God wants." His eyes searched mine. I felt that he wanted to know how seriously to take my words. I continued, "Lupe told me about a little boy in Rachel's condition who was taken home. After four years, he's still living."

"And using a respirator?"

"Yes, and in the same condition. Wilf, I don't want that for Rachel. It frightens me."

"Neither do I, Sandy. Let's talk with Dr. Dayton about this. And, Sandy," he added, "let's think this through carefully. We will come to a good decision." Wilf's voice was steady. I was glad for his knowledge and strength. He squeezed my hand, and I found myself sobbing. Wilf and I were closer together in our thinking than we had been for a long time.

We arranged a community prayer meeting in our home. Many came, and soon our living room was full of people shoulder to shoulder. Every face reminded me of meaningful times we had shared in this close community. Most of the women from my share-group were there, and I saw the concern and sensitivity on their faces. They understood the nature of this meeting and knew of my inner struggle.

Wilf calmly told our friends of Rachel's poor prognosis and the resulting decision facing us. Then he continued, "Sandy and I think the time has come to withdraw the respirator. We want to remove this support gradually. To leave her on the life-supporting machine would only prolong her present condition artificially and indefinitely. The doctors agree that Rachel will not live a normal life, probably never come out of her coma, outside of a miracle. Medically we've done all we can. Now Sandy and I would like to know your thoughts concerning this decision."

We could see tears brimming in the eyes of these close friends and neighbors. It was good to weep in the company of other caring people. One by one they gave us their affirmation of our decision.

Simple prayers were said around the group. Tears flowed freely. Together we were freeing Rachel, trusting God. Maybe he would still heal her; we were helpless to do so. I began to let go and quit demanding of God.

After prayer we sang, accompanied by guitar. Our final song, "God Gives His People Strength," seemed appropriate for our difficult decision.

We felt covered by prayers and love. After singing, Wilf expressed our gratitude. He wanted everyone to know that both of us were all right. Wilf and Jim embraced. Susie and I hugged. Others lingered, comforting us. Why did it often take a crisis to help people touch each other?

9

A Mother's Grief

Hearing a commotion down the hall, I looked toward the door. Just then a nurse rushed in. "Another near-drowning victim is being brought up from the emergency room," she reported.

I felt sick. I watched them wheel the bed into the room with the respirator and intravenous lines already connected to the little boy's body. He was only 20 months old. His small chest was moving up and down in an unnatural manner. The parents were quiet, their faces filled with fear as they stood beside their son.

What could be said to comfort these parents at a time like this? Nothing. The thought of these parents going through the pain we had experienced from the beginning was nearly unbearable. The vividness and ugliness of Rachel's accident again flashed through my mind. I needed to go home and be with Wilf. Together we asked for God's help for these newly stricken parents.

Arriving at the hospital the following morning, I stopped at the nurses' station. Lupe told me that Rachel had been moved to a private room; she no longer needed the respirator. I had anticipated this, but somehow felt unprepared to accept it. Since she could breathe on her own, would she live on indefinitely? I was not ready to face that possibility.

"Lupe, how's the little boy in ICU?"

"He's not doing well, Sandy. The neurologist checked his EEG this morning. It's flat, no sign of any activity."

"Oh, no!" *God, why do these things have to happen?*

When I saw Rachel sleeping peacefully, breathing without the respirator, I thought, *maybe now Jesus will heal her.* But in my heart I knew it would not happen.

After staying with Rachel in the morning, I went home to be with Phillip and Wilf. Wilf had completed his residency, and he would be at home for a month before beginning private practice. My parents, still with us after three weeks, went to the hospital to be with Rachel. *What would normal family life be like again? Or could it ever be normal?*

After putting Phillip to bed for a nap, Wilf and I sat on the sofa in the living room. We talked of Rachel, of her present condition, and of moving her to a different facility. Later we might bring her home with us.

As I walked into Rachel's hospital room that afternoon, I saw a lady leaning on Rachel's bed rail, staring at her. I recognized her as the young grandmother of the little boy in ICU. She turned around and, seeing me, asked, "Is your daughter going to live?" Her face was drawn and frightened.

"I don't know," I replied. "If she does, she will not be normal."

"How long has she been like this? How did it happen?"

As I told her our story, I was filled with a strange new peace about our own situation, but I was saddened by the thought that her grandson would not live. After she left, I sat alone with Rachel. I searched for something to say to this family who would no longer see life in their child. *Do they know the truth or are they hoping so desperately that they cannot hear what the doctors are saying?*

The boy's mother came to the door. I recalled that tired and dazed expression.

"Come in. I'm Sandy."

She walked to the bedside quietly. "I'm Pat," she replied. "My mother told me about your little girl. I'm so sorry," she continued. "I don't know what will happen with Chris. Another EEG is to be done tomorrow."

We each told of our child's accident. I went on to tell her what else had happened since Rachel was brought to the hospital and how we had depended on God's strength, even with all the questions. She listened attentively.

"We live nearby, Pat. You're welcome to come take a shower and rest at our house." She accepted my invitation and seemed to appreciate the break. After she had freshened up, Pat joined my mother and me at our round oak table. Pat talked quietly about Chris. I wanted to take

66

away her pain, the despair I knew she would continue to have for a long time.

The following morning at the hospital, I saw Pat and other members of her family gathered around Christopher's bed. Their weeping told me he had died. How suddenly his death had come. I wished for this family the kind of comfort we were finding.

Rachel's forever existence became more of a reality. No longer was it merely what I could see and feel with my human, temporal senses. No longer could I try to control God and demand the physical presence of a little girl he had not promised I could possess. She was with us for only a few years—but her spirit would continue forever. Strangely, I was becoming free of my *need* to cling to Rachel. I began to relax in God's omnipotence.

Rachel stayed for two weeks in a private room. Her condition remained unchanged. Not knowing how long she would live and not yet feeling capable of caring for her ourselves, we decided to place her in a special nursing home.

We visited a home prepared to take care of eight young physically and mentally handicapped children. It was directed by a registered nurse who had prepared a large room of her house for this purpose. The visit helped us make our decision. The director, Dixie, was warm and friendly, and her home was cheerfully decorated.

When the morning arrived for us to move Rachel, Wilf asked my father to help me. Dad and I drove to the hospital in silence. Nothing much was said as we gathered her belongings—the many gifts and the dresses with simple ties Susie had especially made for use in the hospital.

Dad lifted Rachel out of bed, her thin legs now stiff, her head twisted toward one side. As he carried her quietly down the stairs, the nurse and I walked beside him with her belongings. Through her tears the nurse said, "I love Rachel very much." I thanked her and told her how much I appreciated all she and the other nurses had done.

The car was parked near the bottom of the steps. As my father gently set Rachel on her favorite blanket in the back of our station wagon, I saw him in a new way, as Rachel's grandfather—her Papa. I felt a sadness for him. This was his first grandchild—the little girl he had taken to a park just two months ago. Together they had shared a beautiful day, petting the donkeys, going on the merry-go-round, feeding the ducks, and riding in a boat. Now I watched him lovingly, sadly putting his Rachel into the car to take her to a place where she would not get better.

10

The Promise

The wheat danced slowly in the Oregon breeze while the sun darted in and out of clouds, enhancing smiling faces. My thoughts wandered homeward toward Wilf and Rachel. Wilf had encouraged me to travel to Oregon with my parents to attend my brother Dave's wedding. He thought it would be good for me to get away. Yet now, as often happened since Rachel's accident, I felt out of place, as if I were in a foreign land.

Phillip had come with me and was consistently content. His health and exuberance were reassuring; he was my link with normalcy. The outdoor setting seemed perfect for Dave and his bride, Kathleen. They loved nature and its informality. As I watched the festivities, however, I found myself having to fight back a rising anger: *Life is going on in spite of Rachel—how dare it!*

I remembered the special tenderness Dave had felt for Rachel, his first niece. I was grateful for the smile he gave me when I first arrived in Oregon and the empathy evident in his eyes. He shared some of my pain even in his present happiness. The decision to go ahead with the wedding had been a difficult one.

The clicking cameras reminded me that I also held one. Adjusting the aperture, I was glad for my brief art and photography background which helped me concentrate on the scenes. Throwing myself into a lighter mood, I walked around this strange land of joy, trying to understand and speak its language.

I looked at the interesting face and frame of my Uncle Grant—his strong bone structure and thick white beard. Yesterday he had given me an understanding hug. His wife of many years had died recently.

Kathleen's uncle, also a shutterbug, glanced my way. Last night he had encouraged me to talk of Rachel and had offered me the healing of his empathetic listening.

I continued to search for intriguing expressions and spontaneous moments with my camera. The fun of capturing candid photographs freed me from my gloomy introspection.

A flute solo initiated the ceremony. The high, delicate notes enhanced the beauty of this outdoor scene. Everything and everyone seemed touched by God's caress.

As I looked down the row of seats and saw another uncle of mine whose wife had died several years ago, I noted that the loss of a loved one is a common experience, although rarely discussed, and that most of the people here were not strangers to my emotions.

With affection I watched my brother Mark confidently take his place next to Dave. He had listened well at lunch the day before as I had poured out leftover frustrations and regrets I had bottled inside.

My fatigue and feelings of separation from the others began to lighten. For a moment I supposed the wedding had been planned especially for me, to help lift my spirits.

The crescendo of the flute solo announced Kathleen's entrance. She walked toward Dave, her face alight with joy, the sunshine mixing with her smile. Just six years earlier, Wilf and I had exchanged our lifetime promises, not knowing what the years would bring. Our relationship had wobbled at times, yet, in the face of contrary winds, our bond had grown stronger. What was ahead for Kathleen and Dave?

I was becoming aware of a new realization: I had to release Rachel from myself and from this world. In my prayers I had given her to God, but as a mother to finally resign, "Here, God, she's all yours," was the most difficult task I had ever faced. Rachel was God's gift to Wilf and me. I felt an instinctive possession.

Then her atrophied and stiffened body flashed before me. *Must Rachel die? Must she? Must I release her?* Yes, I knew she was in God's hands, and I believed she would live forever, but I ached inside. I focused on the beautiful wheat fields and remembered, ". . . except a grain of wheat fall into the ground and die. . . ."

Dave and Kathleen were tenderly, solemnly exchanging

71

vows. I prayed for them. My eyes met my parents' faces. I knew they were praying for me as well. The air was filled with blessing and hope. I was bathed in promises. I knew Rachel's death would not be wasted. I caught a glimpse of life as a series of deaths and births for which we are being continually prepared with every breath we inhale and exhale, every time we sleep to arise, with each good-bye.

"You may kiss the bride." The minister was no longer solemn. I yearned for Wilf to be there with me so I could reach over and touch him, but we were miles apart. Dave and Kathleen sealed their vows while the golden wheat in the surrounding fields applauded silently in the wind.

I began my trip home filled with fresh determination, convinced of the promise of beauty that could someday emerge from the grain of wheat. All the way home I kept thinking of Rachel. I knew Wilf and his family had visited, yet a part of me felt I had abandoned my daughter. The same afternoon we arrived home, Mom and I drove to Dixie's.

As we entered the cheerfully decorated room, a hope flickered that Rachel might be better. Dixie, the nurse director, was propping pillows behind the back of a motionless young girl in a wheelchair. Then she ran a brush through the girl's straight blond hair. "Good afternoon, ladies!" she greeted us. "I'm getting Rachel ready for some sunshine. It's a lovely day!"

Suddenly Oregon, the wedding, and promises seemed very far away. I felt weak as recognition grew to horror.

Rachel!! Something in me protested. *That's not my child,* I thought; *that can't be Rachel!*

She was incredibly thin. Her head was turned awkwardly to one side. Her eyes gazed blankly. There was no soft child beauty about her.

I heard a sigh. "Who was that?" I asked.

"Rachel," Dixie answered. "She sighs and makes grunting noises. Dr. Dayton says it's not unusual for this to happen as the swelling in her brain subsides. She's swallowing on her own now."

Did this mean she might come out of her coma? Then what?

My mother began talking to Rachel. "Your grandma and your mommy are here, Rachel. We love you very much."

Are you there, Rachel? I thought to myself. *Can you hear? Are you waiting to be released from this outer shell which is no longer you?*

Mom continued talking quietly to Rachel about our trip and the wedding.

"Sandy, you'll get used to taking Rachel places with you —shopping or to the park," Dixie remarked.

Never! I shouted inside. I wanted to tell this kind nurse that Rachel once was different, that when I took her shopping people stopped and stared, not because her appearance was strange, but because she was beautiful, lively, and friendly. I wanted to tell her about the time, just before the accident, when Rachel went to visit a dying man and made him smile with delight.

Tears began to wet my cheeks as I leaned toward my

helpless child awkwardly propped up in the wheelchair. I stroked her hair. *Yes, you are my Rachel, different now. But God will someday give you a new body. You will be whole again, alive for all eternity.* I kissed her cheek and whispered in her ear, "I love you, Rachel."

11

Rachel Comes Home

For two days in July, Wilf and I stayed in a friend's cabin high in the Sierra Mountains. We took long walks hand in hand—in love, loved. We were sometimes silent. The things we had to say would not fit into words.

We looked closely at the forest. The world seemed recreated in the gentle fingers of the calm fir, in the simplicity of pine needles, from the timid seedlings to the tops of the king sequoias. Tips of branches stretched and begged for heaven, worshiping, longing. Some of the trees were marred—disfigured by time, wind, fire, people—yet still they worshiped. All of the forest, it seemed, was on tiptoe, anticipating. . . . We reached up and almost touched God. He reached out and touched us.

Our favorite music filled the cabin: Chopin, Brahms,

Beethoven's Fifth Symphony. We laughed over numerous games. Laughter came easily. So did tears.

We packed those mere two days with weeks of life—life which we had been afraid or unable to give to each other. Then, as Wilf guided the car down the winding mountain road, we decided that Rachel should come home. Not knowing how long Rachel would live, nor how well we would handle it, we were both relaxed and ready to accept the future together. We wanted her with us—at home.

A crib was set up in Rachel's own room. Other preparations were made for her homecoming. Once again, Rachel lay in the back of our station wagon. As we drove up our driveway, I did not want any neighbors to see us. They would all know soon, but this was a family time, to me a sacred occasion. We were bringing home our daughter whom we deeply loved. She no longer looked like the active child they knew. Maybe I wanted to preserve Rachel's former identity, or perhaps I wanted to shield them from seeing her—or maybe I wanted to protect myself from their response.

Wilf carried Rachel upstairs. He placed her gently, lovingly in the crib in her room, tucking her favorite blanket around her thin body. Together we looked at her for a long moment. Then, spontaneously, we hugged each other, knowing we had made a good decision. Our Rachel was home.

The days that followed became more of a routine. My parents returned to Orange County. Wilf began private practice. Phillip played happily as I cared for Rachel's needs. He easily accepted his sister back. At times he interrupted his activities to watch me bathe, dress, or feed her. One morning he pushed his stool next to her crib. Putting his chubby little hand through the rails, he tickled her feet, laughing. I was glad he was oblivious to Rachel's condition, but I was saddened by the realization that she could not respond.

A week had passed since we brought Rachel home. This particular day I was alone with Rachel. I lifted her rigid body out of the crib and sat with her in a rocking chair. I tried holding her closely but could not; her muscles would not cooperate. I began to sob bitterly as I looked at her silent face. There was no sign of personality, no response. *Rachel!* I wanted to scream, *Wake up! Do something! Why do you stay this way?*

I tried to be still inside and pray. At first the words refused to come. Finally I prayed, "Jesus, please do something. I don't think you intend to heal her. Please release her from this life so she can be completely whole." I sat there a long while, stroking her hair, talking to Jesus.

The following day Wilf's parents and his sister Beverly came over for an evening meal. After supper Mom and I washed the dishes. Wilf's piano music and Bev's pleasing voice filled the house with warmth. Then, as she folded the dish towel, Mom said, "Sandy, I want to be with Rachel."

While she went up the steps to Rachel's room, I blew up a balloon for Phillip. He played happily as Dad and I visited above the music. "Would you like a cup of coffee?" I offered.

"Yes, that would be nice—a little milk in it, please."

I prepared his coffee and set it down on the lamp table. As I turned around, I saw Mom coming down the stairs, her countenance glowing. "Rachel hears her daddy's beautiful music." Mom spoke calmly. "She's ready to leave us. We want her to be completely with God."

Wilf and Bev joined us in the living room. Everyone sat down. It was a solemn moment. In awe of what I had heard Mom say, I studied her face. Just yesterday, while holding Rachel in my arms, I had prayed she be released from this life. Now Mom, who had resisted this thought before, was also ready.

Dad's voice brought me back to the present. "Yes, it is time."

The following morning, on August 18, 1976, while I was quietly feeding her, Rachel died.

12

Saying Good-Bye

I phoned Wilf at his office. When he arrived at home with his partner, Dr. Janzen, his eyes were red from crying. Now that Rachel's death was final, he could no longer contain his emotions.

We stood side by side looking at Rachel. It was an ordinary hazy day in Fresno. Her departure came as no surprise, yet it was difficult for us to comprehend she truly was gone. The sounds of cars whizzing by and children playing helped remind us that life must go on. In a few hours the energy of people around us gently pushed us into action.

We had already agreed to plan a personal, simple ceremony. Wilf proposed building a casket ourselves from beautiful local redwood, and I quickly agreed. Wilf consulted a neighbor, Bob Friesen, who had comforted us many times. He was eager to assist us, so we went ahead with the project. Bob engineered a simple design. Ralph Tomasian, the outgoing Armenian man next door who frequently helped us with our home's plumbing problems, took Wilf in his pickup truck to select the wood from a nearby lumberyard. Wilf told me how good it felt to personally pick out the best boards, and, more precisely, to do it with a significant friend.

Bob, who lived a block down the street, quickly offered his backyard shop for the construction of the casket. Wilf was surprisingly relaxed as he picked up the phone to call some of our friends in the neighborhood. Many came, including Jim. It was especially good to have Wilf's father and brother, Lloyd, present.

The men worked together, saying very little, but all obviously feeling a satisfaction that they were doing something tangible with their hands. If any were apprehensive initially, their apprehensions were soon dissipated by the profound assurance that this working together was somehow sharing Wilf's grief. The same day that Rachel died, our friends and family were working and sharing a meal with us, pounding nails and partaking of sandwiches and iced tea. Even the smell of their sweat in that warm, stuffy shop added to the closeness we felt. These people were not afraid to experience a portion of our grief.

The casket looked beautiful, its brass screws and handles shining boldly. Susie and I put on the finishing touches by lining it with soft, white, quilted material trimmed with red bows. We both felt the love and closeness between us as we worked. I was at peace.

Later that evening, Wilf stopped next door to see Jim. He wanted Jim to know that his presence at the shop was deeply appreciated; it showed courage and caring. Wilf reassured Jim that he loved him.

The personnel at a nearby funeral home were willing to help us in any way they could, readily accepting our need for only a part of their customary services. For us it was a good combination of personal, alternative choices and professional services that made it possible for us to experience an active participation in the final events of Rachel's life. Because she was so close to us, we wanted these events to represent us and others who had loved her.

The next day, Thursday, most of my family arrived. A simple funeral and memorial were planned. I sensed the Spirit of God in the teamwork and harmony of all the people, many from our church, who generously gave of their time to plan and put together these services.

Friday, the day of Rachel's funeral, I wore a white blouse and a long, colorful skirt. Wilf wanted me in something cheerful. At the funeral home, we gently put Rachel's body in her personal casket. It was Wilf's decision to lead the procession with our station wagon, carrying the casket with us in the back of the car.

The funeral-burial ceremony was very short, and the entire service was held outdoors. Gary, the neighbor who had given a speech welcoming us into the neighborhood, spoke of Rachel's life as he had observed it. His special love for children was apparent in his simple, meaningful words. Pastor Janzen, pastor from the church in which

Wilf grew up, spoke of her new life in heaven. "Jesus Loves Me," her favorite song, was sung by all.

When the casket was opened, I was startled to see the thinness of Rachel's body. She did not look like our daughter. I felt overwhelmed with pain for a moment as I put my hand on her arm. Her skin was so cold. Her physical death was indeed a reality. Rachel was no longer a part of this life; she was on a new adventure we would someday share. We had almost decided to keep the casket closed, but I was glad we had opened it. It reminded many of us that Rachel was no longer in her body, that she had said good-bye to earth.

The cousins Rachel had adored were sharing in this ceremony. I noticed one of Rachel's friends, Julie, a lovely, dark-haired, mature nine-year-old. Her expression was one of deep thought.

The following day, friends and relatives joined us at the church for a memorial for Rachel. The chairs were arranged in a semicircle facing a painting symbolizing worship. We, too, were here to worship and to hold out open hands to release our gift of almost three years.

The minister prayed, "Teach us to value the moments we have with each other. . . ." I was quiet inside, yet somewhat numbed by the finality of Rachel's physical death. It was difficult to believe I would never again look at her in this life.

Joy and sadness mingled with the hushed, mellow guitar as we once again sang the promise "God Gives His People Strength." My father stood and spoke calmly of Jesus blessing the children, of Jesus telling us to come to God with a child's heart. Beverly, Wilf's sister, sang "Give Them All to Jesus" lovingly through her tears. By this time many were weeping. It was a good release.

There was a time for sharing. My brother Dave stood and, through his brokenness, said, "God gives us, through children, a glimpse of his intended creation—an awareness of the other side. To me, Rachel was a glimpse of God's perfection; she is a link for us to those who have gone ahead."

"Rachel's life was full of love," my mother said. "Rachel knew how to love freely because she experienced it around her."

"I have always come back to Psalm 23," Wilf's father spoke in his beautiful, deep voice and soft German accent. " 'The Lord is our shepherd'—and he's Rachel's shepherd. We must go to him. And even if Rachel did sleep with her feet in my face the last time she stayed with us, I still love her!"

We all laughed. One by one, friends or family members continued to share.

"Many have talked about Rachel being sweet and good," another friend said. "I took care of her several times. It impressed me that she had a terrible temper when she thought she was facing some injustice. There were times when she would get so angry that she would hold her breath to the extent of passing out."

Wilf chuckled.

She continued, "I think all of us, as we think about our children, are concerned what kind of impact they will have in the world. The world will be without the passion for justice Rachel could have given."

I was glad we were not making Rachel into a little "angel."

"Wilf and Sandy let Rachel spend many times with us," Mom Derksen said. "Yes, she certainly had a strong will. She also was full of life—just like her daddy when he was a young boy. He never could sit still!"

Everyone laughed and looked at Wilf. He had been known by many of the people in the room from his childhood days.

Mom Derksen continued, "The Sunday before Rachel fell into the pool, she came to visit with her daddy. I wanted to ask if I could keep her, but I knew she and Wilf were having such a good time. They often had long conversations together. Theirs was a special relationship. Then Monday—it happened."

Gary, our neighbor, stood to tell of the basket of flowers the neighborhood children had presented to us. He reminded us that we could no longer give physical love to Rachel, yet there were other children around to whom we could offer love.

Dr. Janzen, Wilf's fellow pediatrician and partner, stood up and looked at Wilf for a few moments before speaking. "Wilf," he began slowly, "Rachel is gone." He paused. "But you will see her again and again. You will see her at the office and at the hospital. Time after time, you'll see a charming, sweet, two- or three-year-old girl who reminds you of Rachel. As you do, extra gentleness and kindness

84

will flow from you to her. And you will have a tender place for parents who face loss. And that is good, Wilf."

The time of remembering together was sealed with another song. A thoughtful church committee had prepared sandwiches and salads for lunch. The usual hum of laughter and good talk filled the fellowship room as we ate heartily. I was glad these common pleasures could be enjoyed on such a day—they represented the fact that life would go on.

13

Strange Emotions

Three weeks had passed since Rachel's memorial. The immediate peace and numbness of that time was wearing off. The house grew empty and lonely. Nothing took away the pain of Rachel's absence. Everything I saw or did somehow reminded me of her. I would wash the dishes and see, through the kitchen window, the empty blue lining of the pool next door—vaguely visible through the bamboo fence —and remember. I would see her a hundred times lying by that pool.

I would go through all the if-onlys:

> If only she had been familiar with water—
> If only I had checked in with Susie—
> If only I had just looked sooner—
> If only—

Rachel's footsteps no longer pattered up and down the stairs. Where was she when I reached down to kiss her goodnight?

How long, Lord, will this ache, this heaviness remain? Yes, I know she lives on, but I want to mother her. God, why did Rachel have to leave? Was I not doing an OK job? Maybe I should not have let her out of my sight. But I loved the way she was becoming so independent and inquisitive. Why did she die when family life was at its best? Where were you, God, while we fumbled so carelessly? Did you desire her more than we? Lord, when will I remember without pain? Some days I can handle it. I think the worst has passed, that now I can cope, and then—

One morning, six weeks later, I sat down at my cluttered rolltop desk. On one side were cards and letters sent to us by thoughtful friends and relatives. I had not been able to read with much comprehension before. I picked up a card to read again, hoping for some kind of consolation. At the end of the verse printed on the card was a written message:

> We are sure you will agree that our Lord was kind and good to take your beloved Rachel home to heaven. Rachel is with the Lord Jesus. She no longer has to stay in this sinful world. Rachel must be happy and praising our Lord.

I was furious. I felt a stab pass through me as I read it. How much happier *I* would be if God had chosen to *heal* Rachel. If I had wanted to protect her from this sinful world, I would not have given birth. Rachel had eternity to sing and praise God. It was not necessary for her to leave this earth. I wanted to shout, *Rachel was my daughter! I was her mother! How can anyone say she's better off gone?*

I struggled with my emotions. How could I believe God planned Rachel's accident, that it was in his "perfect will"? I was not sure I believed in a "perfect will." Maybe God continually took our mistakes and conformed them to his will.

I reached for another letter and found one from a well-meaning person whom I had not seen in some time. Part of the letter was not helpful. Even though the words might have been true, I felt angry as I read: "God knew you were strong and he has allowed this trial to happen to you. His grace is sufficient."

How can she assume I am accepting God's grace to give me strength? We have not seen each other for a long time. What if I am not coping and no longer believe in God?

Just then I heard the spontaneous exclamations of happy children playing upstairs. Three neighborhood girls were with Phillip in the playroom—Rachel's room. I heard two-year-old Jodi come downstairs. I looked up smiling, but my smile quickly faded. She had put on and haphazardly buttoned Rachel's red dotted swiss dress, a dress I had folded lovingly and carefully put away. She looked very pleased.

I felt dizzy with sudden anger. Jodi was wearing my daughter's dress and smiling. She wanted to show me. How could she know I wouldn't like it? She thought I would be pleased. I wanted to tear the dress from Jodi, but I reminded myself that Jodi was only doing what Rachel might have done.

"Jodi," I called, trying to be gentle. "Jodi, I see you know how to dress yourself like a big girl. You look pretty. But let's put the dress away now. I'll come help you."

Jodi no longer looked happy. "I want my mommy."

"She'll be here soon. Let's go upstairs now, Jodi." I tried to control my feelings, but when I reached the room, I was furious! Rachel's clothes were everywhere!

"Why are you children making such a mess? You have plenty of playthings. These are not toys! These are Ra—"

The words tumbled out before I could stop them, but then I caught myself, realizing they did not understand. Phillip, the youngest, looked bewildered and on the verge of tears. I went over to him and lifted him into my arms.

I regretted my outburst. After all, these were only pieces of cloth. The children were merely exploring—as—as Rachel might be doing—if—

How many more of these ordinary moments would churn within me, these strange emotions? Daily life began to be unbearable. I needed to talk, to tell of Rachel. I sensed that others felt it was time to go on, to not dwell on the past. Wilf could not talk of Rachel easily; he hurt too deeply. We were unable to tell each other our feelings; the pain was too great and we were in two different places.

Finally I went to Doc's office, knowing I could pour out my heart to him. While waiting, I wrote:

> What is happening to my emotions? These feelings I can't express? Sometimes I just want to scream, scream at

the top of my lungs because I don't know how to say it, I want to be free again—free to run and laugh, to be me. But I don't know who I am anymore. Did part of me drown with Rachel?

In Doc's office, I shifted nervously on the cushioned chair facing him. "Doc, sometimes I feel like I'm unable to handle the simplest situations. I went to my art class this morning and during the class I began thinking of Rachel. I imagined how nice it would be to have a portrait of her. When the class ended, I stopped and asked the instructor if he could suggest an artist. I told him of Rachel, of her death. He gave me the names of a few artists but said nothing at the mention of her death. I felt uneasy, unable to respond."

Doc was attentive as I continued. "We've had a couple staying at our house. When I showed the woman through the house, she saw a photograph of Rachel. When I told her the picture was of our daughter who died a month ago, she said, 'Oh,' and that was all. Can't I tell anyone about Rachel? I want to! I need to talk about her." I was on the verge of tears as I spilled out the accumulated anger and frustration welling within me.

"People go on about their business as if nothing happened. It's as if they were pretending that Rachel had never lived." Sobs shook my body. I felt so helpless, so powerless. "Doc, you know about death—you've experienced losing someone close to you."

Doc's mother, two teenage friends, and Rachel had all died within the same month. Several days ago we had talked on the phone. He had shared with me how afraid he was even to answer the phone, afraid that someone else he loved might have died.

"It's so unfair, Doc, it's so unfair! Doesn't God care?" For the first time in days, I was expressing my anger to another human being. Somehow, in Doc's office, it was safe to express, to experience, to be, without being put down or judged. My mind went back to one of our first counseling sessions. Doc had pointed out that the Bible talks of two kinds of confessions: confession to God for forgiveness, and, in James 5:16, confession to each other for healing. Just being able to express the unacceptable was like a load being lifted off my shoulders.

"Sandy," Doc's voice was reassuring as he leaned forward. His words were kind. "People don't know what to say when there is a death. They care but they are afraid—afraid of saying something stupid. So they say nothing, or they offer a trite cliché or statement, hoping it will be appropriate. They are waiting for us to make it safe for them to ask questions or to express their own emotions."

"Well, I did tell the woman about Rachel in an offhand manner, almost flippantly, I guess. And I suppose the art instructor couldn't have known how important that picture of Rachel was to me."

"People often don't know what we are feeling until we tell them. All they can do is guess. And when it comes to death, most people are afraid of guessing. It's too dangerous. If we want them to share with us, we have to make it safe for them."

Doc's words made sense to me. I had known that others were waiting for me to bring up the subject of Rachel, but

I hadn't liked the role. I didn't want to take the responsibility. Somehow there was a part of me that said that if they really cared, they would know what I needed, they would know how to respond. I realized I had put unrealistic expectations on others.

"It is safer not to say anything, not to open up the conversation." Doc touched my hand. "But if we want people to reach out to us, we must reach out to them to help them deal with their own fear—their own fear of death and the fear of saying the wrong thing."

Now I understood that I needed to verbalize my feelings regarding Rachel to others, whether people responded or not. I looked at the poster on Doc's wall, and for the first time I understood: "Resentments come from the repression of feelings, not the expression of feelings." Now I could stop blaming others for not guessing right, for not being able to read my mind. But I had more to tell now that I was letting some of the feelings surface.

That afternoon I went to Grace's house.

"Grace, I'm so angry I don't know what to do!" Tears welled up in my eyes as I pounded my fist on the arm of the plaid couch.

Grace sat across from me in an overstuffed chair. "Sandy," she said calmly, "tell me more."

"I don't know what to do with all my negative feelings."

"What makes you angry, Sandy, or who?"

My eyes were hot with tears. I felt my fists clench. I was afraid I would explode if I opened my mouth. Finally I spoke. "I hate feeling this way. I keep blaming Susie, Jim, myself—all of us—for Rachel's accident. If only we had been more careful, if only we had made other choices. It didn't have to happen. Why Rachel? Why didn't God make us more aware?"

"Sandy, you're angry at many people, even yourself and God. But maybe you need to begin by understanding why you're angry at Jim and Susie."

"I know I shouldn't be angry with them. It could have occurred anywhere. It just happened to be in their yard."

"But you are angry, Sandy. You can't just make a feeling go away by saying 'shouldn't.' "

"Grace, I love Susie. But we don't even talk anymore. No one person is to blame for Rachel's death. But I can't handle how I feel toward myself or Susie or Jim. And, Grace, God seems so far away."

"Sandy, I can accept your feelings. Think how much more God loves and understands you. He knows you're angry. You can't hide it from him. Tell God how you feel —he can handle it."

For a few moments I sat quietly, weighing her words.

"What is Wilf feeling?" Grace questioned gently.

"Oh, he doesn't blame anyone," I blurted. "He aches terribly. His experience of Rachel's loss is different from mine. It's difficult to share with him how I feel because he isn't angry like I am. I need to remember her life. I want to look at her pictures and listen to her voice on tape. That's not helpful to him. His pain is worse when he remembers.

"There have been times when Wilf has questioned his ability to continue living. I want to help him but don't know how. He's often very quiet when he's home in the evenings. And I need him to listen to *me!*"

"Sandy, you're both hurting, even if in different ways. It's not easy for you to comfort each other. Talking with others you know and trust will ease Wilf's burden of meeting all your needs. If he could do the same, the two of you would grow stronger and more able to comfort each other."

14

A Path to Healing

That night I paced up and down the sidewalk in front of Susie and Jim's house. The stars flickered impersonally. Wilf was at the hospital working. Friends were watching Phillip.

I needed to speak with Jim and Susie, but I was afraid. Would it make the situation worse? I had to take that risk. I was already hurting them by not talking. Doc's words came to me again. "The opposite of love is not anger. Often we become angriest at those we love most."

It was difficult to walk to the front door. Maybe they would hate me for telling them how I felt. The scene of Rachel's accident became vivid once again—her helpless body beside the pool. A young, innocent life wasted! If only we had been more aware!

Finally I rang the doorbell. Jim answered. His eyes seemed expressionless. He said hello in an empty voice.

"May I come in?" I asked nervously. "I need to talk with you and Susie."

"Sure, come in." He looked uneasy.

I sat down in the family room. Susie came out of the kitchen. Her eyes were sad and questioning. "I'll be right there."

Jim and I were both quiet, waiting for Susie. We could not look at each other. When Susie walked in and sat across from me, we were all very tense. Finally I spoke. My voice shook. "The last few weeks have been very difficult. I can't stop thinking about Rachel. The events of her accident keep going through my mind. I think of all the ways her horrible death could have been prevented. I'm beginning to feel very resentful toward both of you. I know it's not right, but it's the way I feel. Can you understand?"

They nodded.

My voice became stronger, but it still shook. "Susie, I don't want to blame you—what happened was not your fault. Jim, I know you were not intentionally careless by not covering the pool, but Rachel's gone, and I feel upset and angry at both of you. If only we all would have been more careful."

They listened quietly. Surprisingly, they did not become defensive. I tried to look at Jim but I could not meet his eyes directly.

"Jim, if only you had put a cover on that pool! It

wasn't protected! I know you had good intentions and didn't think it was dangerous—it was so shallow.

"And, Susie, I know it's not fair to put blame on you when I didn't even make it definite I wanted you to watch Rachel. You thought she had come home—Oh, I love both of you and I can't stand it that we haven't been talking! I don't want that to continue."

I was amazed how relieved and relaxed I was beginning to feel and how quickly the anger was disappearing. Now I wondered how Jim and Susie were feeling.

Susie looked so hurt. "I think I understand how you feel, Sandy, but I don't think it's fair for you to blame us. You know I would never have left Rachel if I hadn't thought she was in your house. I think about Rachel all the time and cry for her. How can you think I'd be so careless when I felt so close to Rachel?" She was crying.

"I know, Susie; I know you loved Rachel deeply. And she loved being with you." It struck me that perhaps Susie was still unable to let go of Rachel.

"This could have happened anywhere," Jim was saying. "Many pools much larger than ours are left unprotected." I thought of a number of pools around the neighborhood, and I knew he was right. And the pool had just been filled the night before the drowning. "I *had* planned to put a cover on it soon," he continued, "but in order to get the lining to stay down, I had to fill it with water."

"We wanted it to be so special," Susie added, "a happy place for the neighborhood children. We had no idea it would turn out this way! Jim had spent hours preparing it very carefully. It was only a foot and a half deep."

"It's difficult to believe that a pool so shallow could be so dangerous," I responded.

Susie said, "I've wanted to talk with you many times, but I didn't know how. I'm glad you came over." Jim nodded in agreement.

Before I fell asleep that night, I placed an entry in my journal:

> . . . such a relief and the load is gone! An odd thing has happened—I don't feel angry anymore. Or is it so odd? I've found the maxim to be true: negative feelings expressed often lose their power. It is good to feel Susie and Jim's caring and to be close to them again. Now I understand, "Be angry, but sin not . . . . "

Deep healing had begun.

The morning was dew-fresh. I sat outside, lingering in the early quietness, trying to make it last. I had been through weeks of confusion and continual dull aching; there had been piercing stabs of remembering, guilt, and even bursts of anger. Now many of these emotions had passed.

My preoccupation with the shortness of Rachel's life had caused me to experience a deep sense of futility—an emptiness. But now I had told God of my anger and frustrations and had felt his understanding and acceptance. As Grace had said, he could handle it.

This morning as I relaxed in still gladness, experiencing his presence, I felt a new freedom. Expressing my deepest emotions with friends had provided an avenue to a more open, more intimate communion with God my Father.

15

Wilf

A letter came from Leroy and Carol Friesen. Leroy would soon be the full-time pastor of our church. I knew neither of them, but Wilf and Leroy had been friends. Carol had written:

> We'd like to know more about Rachel. Sometime I would like to hear about Rachel from you. Even though she isn't a part of your lives any longer, I'm sure it would be good for you to recall special things and events about this person who for nearly three years was a very significant part of your lives.

The invitation to talk about Rachel made me feel an immediate closeness to both Leroy and Carol. When they came to visit us soon after their move to Fresno, I felt at ease with them.

They wanted to see our remodeled old house, and we eagerly took them on a casual tour. In the dining room, Leroy paused to look at pictures of Rachel sitting on the buffet.

Turning to us, he remarked, "It's good to have pictures of Rachel, to remember, to think of her."

"Thank you for noticing, Leroy," I replied. "Seeing her pictures reminds me of her life with us. I don't want to forget."

"You know," Wilf added, "we appreciated the thoughts you and Carol expressed in your letter to us. You wrote of wanting to know more about Rachel."

"Yes, we do want you and Sandy to tell us the things about her that are important to you," Carol replied.

"Make yourselves comfortable in the living room," I said, motioning to the adjacent room. "I'll fix some tea."

I could hear the sounds of easy conversation and laughter as I arranged the tea tray. I felt anticipation walking into the living room, appreciating the warmth of Carol and Leroy's presence.

Leroy shifted his position as he poured himself a mug of tea. "What was unique about Rachel, Wilf?"

"She looked like me," Wilf answered laughingly. "Especially when she frowned."

Continuing more seriously, I added, "She was a child who had an intense disposition, a child of many moods. Rachel was also very bright."

"Sandy," Wilf interjected, "almost every mother I see in the office thinks her child is exceptionally bright."

100

Carol laughed easily. "Keep talking, Sandy. We want to hear about her."

"She wasn't always an easy child to parent. Her strong will and energetic spirit needed taming with an abundance of love and understanding."

"The memories of her last six months are vivid. She had become an easier, more peaceful child, chattering or singing continuously," Wilf interrupted. I was glad to hear him finally talking about Rachel.

"What made the difference for her?" asked Leroy.

"Maybe because Wilf and I were happier and Phillip was more content. Wilf was taking more time to be with the children."

"We liked our move to this house in this particular neighborhood where we and our children found friendships and a feeling of belonging so easily," Wilf added.

Changing the tone of the conversation, Leroy looked seriously at me and asked, "What has happened since Rachel's funeral and memorial service? What kind of thoughts have you had?"

"It's been a time of learning to understand myself and God better," I replied. Then I told them of my anger, my talks with Doc, Grace, and Jim and Susie. I continued by saying, "I am finding by expressing my feelings that my life is not consumed with the heaviness of Rachel's loss. I do need others who can listen to me. Because Wilf is hurting too, he is unable to listen and comfort me as others often can. And I don't know how to comfort him." I paused. "It helps to tell you."

"During our three years in the Middle East, we noticed

that the grieving process is treated differently from the way we experience it here," said Carol as she eased back into her chair. "Here we expect our people to get over their grief quickly. It is not easy to talk of death. There people are expected to grieve for a long period of time. They wear mourning clothes, and their family and friends grieve with them."

Wilf began to recall some of his many encounters with death and grief in Nigeria. "That was our experience in Africa. We saw many deaths. Death there was a common fact of life. I discovered that nearly every family in the village had lost at least one child.

"One of the most difficult times for me was the death of two young girls. They died after being badly burned by a cooking fire." As Wilf spoke, I recalled the circumstances of that particular accident.

———◆———

Wilf had just begun rounds on the obstetrical ward at Garkida Hospital when a staff member rushed toward him, speaking rapidly in Hausa. "You are to go to the children's ward, Likita! Two girls—a fire—"

"Please speak English this time; your Hausa is too fast for me."

Wilf turned his complete attention toward the man and learned that the daughters of Malam Kantoma, a hospital co-worker, had been terribly burned. The older daughter had been playing with fire while carrying her younger sister on her back.

When Wilf saw the small girls, aged three and five, he realized that the prognosis was grim. Garkida Hospital was adept and successful at skin grafting, but, in spite of the best treatment, both girls died. Before they died, the girls had to suffer three weeks of several graftings and numerous dressing changes to their tender skin.

For Kantoma, his family, the neighbors, and the village, a mourning period began. The sadness and pain, the details, the period of transition and loss were shared by many.

In Nigeria it was acceptable to weep in the presence of others and God. Day after day, people would leave their farms or other places of work to join a bereaved friend or relative. Privacy and carrying one's own burdens are rare in a country like Nigeria. To the grieving Garkidan, the important thing was the *presence* of caring people.

Malam Kantoma had been close to Wilf as a friend and worker at the hospital. Wilf had much respect for him and his other co-workers. He depended on their skill and experience to help with the overwhelming numbers of inpatient medical and postsurgical patients. It was natural that Wilf would personally share Kantoma's loss.

Why would God, the Lord and giver of life, allow two beautiful daughters of a godly man to die? Just as they began to blossom and taste the joys of earth and family, life was taken from them.

Wilf was not one to ask many questions of God. Somehow that had always seemed so useless—so answerless. But here in Kantoma's home, he felt especially helpless. After all, wasn't he the Likita—the Doctor? Would the daughters have been saved if treated in a modern, well-equipped hospital? Maybe, but maybe not.

A few days later, Wilf went to Kantoma's compound. It was early evening, and everyone else had gone home. Wilf joined his friend in the front entryway. They sat side by side on wooden folding chairs, watching a goat or dog go by and people of all ages coming and going.

Then Wilf placed his hand, tremblingly, on Kantoma's shoulder. "Malam Kantoma, I don't know how you feel. I don't know how to comfort you. Having never experienced such a loss, I just don't understand it. Do you ask why? Do you ask God why he didn't do something? Do you ask questions?"

When Kantoma finally spoke, his warm, sad eyes were glistening with tears. "Likita," he said, "everything is at last in God's hands. I believe him and I trust him. Somehow I know that he is good. The sorrow that wounds my heart is a deep one. I miss my daughters, and I shall continue to do so. The pain is so strong—oh, Likita! The pain is so great!" Here there was a catch in his throat, and Wilf swallowed his own tears.

Kantoma continued, "I don't know if the wounds will ever heal on this earth. But I know I can keep on living. My friends, too, have known this pain. I've seen others suffer, and I've comforted them. Now death has come to me and my house, and we must, with God's help, go on living."

———◆———

Wilf turned to me as he continued, "Thinking about

Kantoma has been a tremendous strength to me, Sandy. He experienced it before me. Now it's our turn. We are not alone in our loss."

Leroy looked at Wilf. "You talk about how others grieve, Wilf, but you are quiet about your own feelings. Sandy talks freely of Rachel and of her loss. For you it seems much more difficult. It must be painful to talk of Rachel."

"Yes, it is." Wilf's face was strained.

Leroy continued looking at Wilf. "Maybe for Sandy it's easier to talk of Rachel because her days, her hours were filled with her. Then Sandy was continually at the hospital, close to her. Perhaps for you, Wilf, all the special times flood back when you come home from work and your emotions are intensified."

Wilf nodded. "Yes, Leroy, it is like that for me. I miss her most at home and try to escape. Sandy has felt a lot of anger toward God and different people; I haven't. It's good for her to work it out, to express her feelings. I don't know what I need. Maybe in time I will know."

"Each of us has a different response to grief; each must do it in his own way." Carol spoke calmly.

I said, "I want to be able to talk with Wilf about this experience we've gone through together. I'm afraid for Wilf—afraid he's not allowing himself to express his feelings."

I turned to Wilf and saw the hurt in his eyes. "But, Sandy, if only I knew how to do it!" He broke down and sobbed softly. "There are many days that I see a little girl in the office who reminds me of Rachel. I often bend down for a gentle embrace, and it moves me so deeply to feel her warmth. That terrible pain of losing Rachel is so intense. It is getting better, but very slowly. I guess it takes a long time."

Leroy put his hand on Wilf's knee. "Sometimes grief is a slow process."

Carol added, "Wilf, we don't all grieve like Kantoma. We don't all grieve like people in Nigeria or the Middle East. Our culture shapes us to some degree in the way we handle grief. But we are individuals, and coping with grief is personal."

I thought of Wilf comforting Malam Kantoma. Now Wilf was receiving consolation from Leroy and Carol, and I received a new understanding of Wilf.

16

Joy and Tears

Dale and Connie rented a cozy cabin home nestled among tall deciduous and evergreen trees on the edge of a small lake on the outskirts of Brevard, North Carolina. It was a place of dreams.

We had been there in the springtime. Now it was the latter part of October. Leaving Fresno to be with two of our favorite people was a welcome change for Wilf, Phillip, and me. The brilliance of the autumn colors enhanced our time together. We would stay awake late playing games or visiting by the fireplace.

One night after all were in bed, Wilf contentedly asleep beside me, I lay wide awake. A sky filled with flickering lights was visible through the window next to the bed. I reflected on the reality of God's creation through the experiences of the day.

It had been a delightful one. We picked apples in a nearby orchard, sampling each variety as we went from tree to tree. Continuous conversation and laughter filled our joyous time together.

Earlier the same morning, through the kitchen window, Phillip could be seen beside his father fishing. There was a serenity and completeness in the picture of father and son silhouetted in the glimmery beauty of the lake.

I cherished watching this scene, yet longed for myself —as a mother—to be with my daughter, Rachel. Last spring we had thrown pebbles in the lake, then wandered down the path to feed the horses. We ran up and down the green hills, pausing to examine wild flowers.

The night was quiet except for the echoing within me. *Rachel is gone.* I lay in bed, trying to turn off the memories. The beauty of life experienced that day caused the intensity of Rachel's loss to seem even greater. I had thought these crippling feelings of loss and pain were over.

"Rachel, where are you?" I cried out. My soul was uneasy. The burden of feeling responsible for Rachel's death became overwhelming. My body shook as I sobbed uncontrollably, guilt flooding my being. The tragedy of Rachel's loss seemed unbearable. I no longer wanted to live.

"Wilf, wake up!" I began to shake him.

"What, Sandy?"

"It's all my fault, Wilf. Rachel's gone. How can I go on living anymore, Wilf? I let Rachel drown."

Wilf held me close to his warm body, allowing me to release my feelings of guilt and emptiness. We cried and talked, letting our acceptance and love for each other heal our brokenness. When I awoke at dawn, it was to a chorus of birds singing—the start of another perfect day.

These times of joy intermingled with tears continued to occur in our lives. On another occasion, one sunny Saturday afternoon the next spring, Wilf announced he would like to visit the cemetery. "I want to stand by Rachel's grave and remember her," he explained calmly. "I want to have a good cry. Phillip must come too, to be with us when we both weep. He is part of what keeps me in touch with the delight of life."

A few minutes later, the three of us were heading down the road in our station wagon toward Reedley Cemetery. Wilf appeared steady and confident as he guided the car. I was quiet, which was rare for me, while Wilf mused further.

"I am happy today, Sandy. Look at those grapevines and peach trees beside the road. They've made it through the winter, and now those promising small green leaves are coming out all over their limbs."

Phillip was stuttering contentedly as he attempted to count the fingers on his hand. Wilf laughed. I wondered how he could feel so buoyant and yet wish to go to a place that represented grief and pain. What a contrast. Somehow, though, I too felt eager. I was ready for this now. I felt surprisingly cheerful.

Wilf became quiet and sober as he turned the car into

the cemetery driveway. Phillip struggled out of his seat restraint and jumped out enthusiastically. He darted among the gravestones and flowers, shouting happily at the birds that risked landing on the nearby bushes and trees.

As Wilf and I walked slowly, hand in hand, I pictured Rachel alive somewhere, in heaven, in a place like the land of Narnia. I could see her running around, exploring everywhere. I had a great longing to see what she was doing. Wilf's firm hand gave me peace.

I held Wilf close as we came upon her engraved name: RACHEL ANN DERKSEN. What a beautiful name. What a lovely person she was—is. It was such a contrast to see Rachel's burial spot in such a serene place and to see Phillip running around, proudly yelling out the numbers and letters he recognized on the surrounding gravestones. He was oblivious to the significance of this place and the solemnness of the moment. We chuckled as we wept, appreciating life, catching Phillip's innocent delight, but feeling the pain of our daughter's loss.

We took a walk, arm in arm, down to the far end of the cemetery where the meandering Kings River separated it from fields and vineyards. We sat down on the grassy bank and watched its lazy flow. It was shallow enough to see little sandbars in the middle, like islands in a miniature kingdom. The birds were singing. Phillip chased them till they flew to another spot on the grass. He laughed as they teased him to pursue them further.

"I am at peace, Sandy, I'm glad to be alive. Life can go on—and I'm eager for what the future holds."

Here we were, the three of us together, and somehow Rachel also was a *living* part of that moment. As Wilf held me very close, I felt profoundly glad.

17

Life Is Eternal

The beauty of the sun-cleansed Easter morning lifted my spirits. Holidays without Rachel were particularly difficult. The discrepancy between my feelings of loss and the joy of the resurrection reopened my wounds. Just seven months before such a tender part of myself had been torn away.

As we drove to church, the fresh spring air blew in through the car window, ruffling Phillip's hair—like Rachel's, straight and golden blond.

Usually when Wilf appeared preoccupied, I kept quiet, but this morning my feelings about Rachel needed to be shared. "Remember those walks you and your daughter would take, Wilf? She waited eagerly for you to get home. The wind makes me think of kites and how she loved to fly them with you."

Wilf's blue eyes deepened. He smiled but was silent.

"Remember how matter-of-factly Rachel sang, 'Jesus Loves Me'? One day at the supermarket she sang that song at the top of her lungs. Shoppers couldn't help smiling. Did I ever tell you about that?"

"I think so," Wilf acknowledged. "Do you realize she looked a lot like me?" he continued, "the forehead, eyes, and hair, right?" He glanced my way teasingly.

"Actually, Wilf, she resembled you in many ways. Your mother was delighted from the start that she looked like a Derksen."

Wilf was obviously pleased.

Arriving at church, we placed Phillip in the nursery and then made our way to the sanctuary. Nearly 200 people sat in a semicircle. We found a place near the front. A rugged, life-size cross rested at a slant against the platform.

Among the familiar faces, I noticed Marlys sitting with the choir. Marlys's and Oscar's five-year-old Melanie had died a couple of years before, soon after Easter. They and this community had watched her die, slowly losing her battle with cancer.

The children sat with their families, looks of anticipation on their faces. All the members of the congregation held fresh flowers cut from their own yards. Nature's fragrance and beauty filled the chapel. Leroy, the pastor, young and powerful of build, invited us to bring our flowers to the cross.

Wilf and I watched while others took their flowers forward. A visiting young lady was pushed in a wheelchair to the cross. I glanced at Marlys, whose Melanie had also been pushed to the cross in a wheelchair on her very last Easter Sunday. I understood the tears in her eyes. Even the sight of a wheelchair or the singing of "Jesus Loves Me" triggered deep, wrenching pain. *Do such wounds ever completely heal?*

I pictured Mary, Jesus' mother, helplessly watching her Son suffer a cruel death on the cross. I sensed a portion of God's agony while Christ died. More than at any other time in my life, I better understood Christ's suffering. As I thought of the long loneliness that Christ must have experienced, I sensed in a new way that he comprehended the precise depth of my pain. Death had been broken by love on a long-ago cross. In this very room, love transcended death and the loneliness of separation.

I placed my azaleas on the left arm of the rough-hewn cross. The Lord of all the world had once died on such a twisted remnant of his own creation. Just the simple act of bringing beauty to the lifeless wooden form pricked through my pain with the promise of hope. Now, in this ceremony, his living presence was with us.

Rachel, how you would have loved bringing your flowers to the cross! But how much more you must understand it now. As tears rolled down my cheeks, I saw Wilf, a few feet from me, alone with his own grief. I longed for his embrace.

When I sat down, Waldo and Rachel Hiebert turned around and squeezed my hands. Often, I have found, healing comes in such small and loving gestures.

After Wilf sat down, he took my hands in his. His

114

reddened eyes met mine. There was a strength and bond between us that emerged from experiencing together the same deep agony, yet, in a sense, each of us grieved alone.

Eagerly the children came forward, encircling the tall pastor. I kept seeing Rachel's face among them. I pictured Jesus welcoming the children in that long-ago meadow. I heard his voice saying, "Let the little ones come to me and don't forbid them, for of such is the kingdom of heaven."

The children and their pastor talked of Christ's death and resurrection. Even some of the youngest had already experienced the loss of close friends of the family.

Leroy spoke to the whole assembly:

> For nearly two thousand years, members of the Christian community have come together on this morning, Easter morning, to confess and celebrate the resurrection of Jesus Christ from the dead.
>
> This day has often had two points of focus. One of these looked to the past, the first century; it centered in God's victory over death in Jesus whom we call the Christ. The second focus has often been toward the future, for Christians have also believed that on the last day, they too would be resurrected in the completion of God's victory over death.
>
> However, this morning I wish to address neither the past nor the future, but rather that thin line moving between them: the present. What does it mean for us here, now, that death has been overcome in Jesus Christ? How does the resurrection get out of the creed and into our lives? What does it mean for us to be Easter persons?

Leroy talked of the Dark Fridays in our lives, the little deaths, the big deaths, the multitude of losses. He spoke

115

of broken relationships. It was a knowing congregation. I looked around at the beautiful faces marked with the memory of pain. *Thank you, Lord, for the communion of your family.*

The pastor mentioned specific losses. As he alluded to our family, we felt love spread across the room and enfold us. He continued:

> There are those of us who have undergone vocational crises which have shaken our sense of worth and self-confidence. During this year there have been those of us whose seemingly sound marriages have been shaken to the foundations. There have been those among us this last year who have risked much in loving others and have been hurt, scarred, and rendered timid by what happened. We have not been strangers to the many faces of death. We have known pain, disappointment, loneliness, emptiness, and despair.

I wondered at the intermingling of sorrow and rejoicing in this life. I felt close to Leroy—felt Christ's arms through him. I was beginning to know, not only with my mind but also with my emotions, that Christ understood my deepest crying.

> . . . The temptation to cite the particular expressions of death in one's own life as an excuse to retreat from living can be very strong. In fact, it may appear seemingly irresistible. I know this well, as do you. It may appear that the life of being at peace is a way reserved for others who have not gone through what you or I have. And yet, the message of this day is that after all of the death words with their tone of finality about them, after all of your own public and

private Dark Fridays, there is one last word, God's word of life.

Leroy paused; his tone became quieter and more thoughtful.

I could well be accused of throwing out easy words, of running at the mouth with cheap talk in a world filled with pain and death, both far away and close to home. I might be accused of seeking to blunt the knife-edge of pain by employing a rosy, romanticized world view. I might be accused of making my peace with the pain of this world by emphasizing the world to come.

But the road to becoming Easter people does not pass through the land where pain and death are disguised and not acknowledged. New life does not emerge out of death for those who deny the reality of that death. Easter is not an escape from Dark Friday. The loss of your child, Wilf and Sandy, is very real, and becoming an Easter family does not mean that you view it as less so. Becoming an Easter person does not take place by acting as if the pain were not there. Easter is not an alternative to Dark Friday: it comes to those of us in whom that darkness is being transformed by the healing power of God's spirit . . . .

. . . The prophet Isaiah wrote of the suffering servant that "by his stripes we are healed." The Church has viewed this text as applicable to Jesus the Christ and has thus believed that his pain and agonizing death were somehow transformed into the source of our life. We have believed that life has come out of death. Christ the healer is the wounded healer. There is no other healer.

The force of the message was clear. Surely this healing process would have to continue for the months ahead.

117

The pain was gradually being displaced by a comforting peace. I was suddenly excited about it. I felt like shouting, "I'm going to be all right, my little daughter!"

Leroy concluded his message:

> God is at work birthing the new and the old out of the pain and chaos of our daily lives. . . . No situation, no person, no relationship is beyond God's ability to transform, redeem, heal . . . the power of God raised Jesus, raises us. . . .
>
> Even in the tombs of our loneliness and despair, God is there. . . . Even in the shadow and silence of winter, the earth is pregnant with the seeds of God's goodness. . . . There is a way of coming at life and at sorrow in which death can be continually defeated.
>
> Life is a gift to be danced . . . let us dance each moment, even in the shadow—especially in the shadow of Enemy Death because Christ is our brother and we are Easter people . . . for we were born on Easter.
>
> Christ is risen! God is inviting us to choose life.

Epilog

Rachel, our firstborn child, has been absent now for five years. Through the events described in this book, and as we looked at the events that followed, we began to see another side of sorrow.

Soon after we were notified this book would be published, I relayed the news to a friend. She enthusiastically replied, "God had a purpose in allowing this tragedy to happen to your daughter."

"No," I objected gently, "I don't believe we need to find reasons to justify our tragedy, but I do believe good can come out of it."

The lessons of life and death I see as a web, fragilely spun, easily unnoticed and brushed aside if one does not stop to examine them. Because of Rachel's death, Wilf and I actively allowed God's touch to bring us to a deeper, more open communion. It was not by denying our feelings, hoping they would pass, but by sharing together and with others. Our sharing these deep emotions with our earthly brothers and sisters enabled us to more freely communicate our feelings with Christ, our Brother. Our faith has become stronger as we have learned to know God better, to understand more fully who he is. Our faith is not based only on what God does or what we think he should do. We have been reminded through experience that "God's ways are higher than our ways." The many questions we once asked can be left unanswered.

Wilf, in his pediatric practice, has cared for a number of children who were injured or died as the result of drowning accidents. At first the pain and sorrow he had experienced with Rachel's loss returned again in full force. In later incidents, however, he has not again felt the pain or grief so intensely, but he has continued to feel a special confidence, calmness, and empathy in relating to parents in similar tragic situations.

The spring following the healing Easter, we desired another child, and we were saddened by the fact that I could no longer bear any children. At the beginning of May we received a call from my obstetrician telling us of a mother who would soon deliver and wanted her child placed in another family. That evening, with the doctor and his wife, Wilf and I joyously celebrated our affirmative decision. Then, on May 4, while Phillip and I were visiting Connie and Dale in North Carolina and Wilf was attending a medical conference in Los Angeles, the doctor called to announce our little boy had been born.

Once flight arrangements had been made to get us home as quickly as possible, Phillip and I took a stroll by the lake. We breathed the fresh, crisp air and were surrounded by the blossoming spring flowers. Just six months before, Wilf and I had visited this very place. At that time I had what I thought were insurmountable feelings of guilt and pain, and I had no longer wanted to live. Now I sensed the whole earth dancing with me, celebrating our new son's birth. On May 6, 1977, Wilf and I, arm in arm, walked into the hospital. Together we met our newly adopted child, Timothy Peter.

In March 1981, during a telephone conversation, Susie asked if we intended to pursue another adoption. A year had passed since we had applied to adopt an older child without success. I replied that we were truly content with our present family, then, with humor, added, "But if someone just happens to call and ask if we would like to adopt a baby, maybe we would reconsider." Three hours later, someone did call. Ten days later, Erica Maria, our newly adopted daughter, was in my arms.

We are not given final conclusions in this life, though we gain insights that keep us looking for them in the tapestry we weave with God. While we see only part of the total design, the pattern grows in value, for our personal costs are great. God holds mysteries we may not come close to penetrating fully, or even partially, but to us he does give themes that reveal meaning to all earthly events.

As I mentioned earlier, in many ways Rachel is still visible to us. In seeing Phillip and Timothy and Erica, we see her too, for she is at the center of the many strands that tie us together as a family. Not only our family, but others who knew Rachel and even those who did not know her, also are affected by her life and death and the thoughts that continue to be reborn in our daily discoveries.

When Susie's third child was born, at home, in the midst of their family, with doctor and midwife in attendance, I was privileged to be present at that very special occasion. At that time, Susie and I witnessed and experienced a needed rebirth together, for part of us had died with Rachel, just as part of her lives on in each of us.

Rachel's sister, Erica, has become the marvelous complement to her two brothers, Phillip and Timothy. Born on the first day of spring, our youngest child is a daughter for this new season of life—hers and ours. As six-year-old Phillip says, "Mommy, now there are four children in our family: two sisters—Rachel in heaven and Erica here—and two brothers—Tim and me."

We must wait now
For a future day,
      when
In some unguessed hour
We again shall meet
  that wide smile,
   star-globed eyes,
Touched then
With some splendor
Not yet in our dreams,
Our elder
In fresh-faced
Unthought
Beauty.

And in the waiting,
We shall see goodness.
     This is
The promise
To we twice born
  who feel pain,
  weep bitter tears,
Find our hearts
In shreds.
To us is given
Light in the dark,

Warmth in
Frosted wilds, A
God who bled.

We are closer now,
The miles gone
The walls crumbled,
Our lives entwined.
   The bodies' pain
   hurts every part,
And we now ache
And heal as one.
Our hands grip tight
Together
The only rock
Who heals our open wounds
And gives us resurrection
            morn.

And with each passing day
We are less tied to this decay,
But find our loves have slipped away
Where we shall come, another day.

Jim Becker, a neighborhood friend
August 1976